This book is dedicated to all migrants, emigrants, and immigrants, to the deported and departed, to those who have left their homes in search of a new one, and faced numerous challenges in order to make a better life for themselves and their loved ones. Thank you for making our world a better place.

UNSUNG AMERICA

Immigrant
Trailblazers
and Our Fight
for Freedom

PRERNA LAL

mango
PUBLISHING

Coral Gables

Published by Mango Publishing Group, a division of Mango Media Inc.

Cover, Layout & Design: Morgane Leoni
Endsheet Art: © Julio Salgado

For permission requests, please contact the publisher at:

Mango Publishing Group
2850 S Douglas Road, 2nd Floor
Coral Gables, FL 33134 USA
info@mango.bz

For special orders, quantity sales, course adoptions and corporate sales, please email the publisher at sales@mango.bz. For trade and wholesale sales, please contact Ingram Publisher Services at customer.service@ingramcontent.com or +1.800.509.4887.

Unsung America: Immigrant Trailblazers and Our Fight for Freedom

Library of Congress Cataloging-in-Publication number: 2019944135
ISBN: (print) 978-1-64250-112-4, (ebook) 978-1-64250-113-1
BISAC: SOC007000 SOCIAL SCIENCE / Emigration & Immigration
        POL070000 POLITICAL SCIENCE / Public Policy / Immigration

Printed in the United States of America.

CONTENTS

• • • • • • • • • • • •

Foreword	6
Introduction	13
The Promise and Peril of Citizenship	22
Deporting Dissent	65
The Immigrant History of Sexuality	111
The New Age of Resistance	187
Afterword	229
Acknowledgments	236
Suggested Contributions	238
Glossary	243
Sources	249
About the Author	312
About Mango	314

FOREWORD

· · · · · · · · · · · ·

The Dream the Dreamers Dreamed
Allegra M. McLeod

On July 4, 2018, Therese Patricia Okoumou scaled the Statue of Liberty in protest of US immigration enforcement tactics, decrying that in this purported democracy "we are holding children in cages." Earlier that week, close to one million people took to the streets across the country condemning the brutality of immigrant detention centers, and earlier that same morning, on the Statue of Liberty's pedestal, the group Rise and Resist had unfurled a banner reading Abolish ICE. As the afternoon wore on, Okoumou, a forty-four-year-old woman born in the Democratic Republic of Congo, sat upon Lady Liberty's robes, and while police helicopters circled overhead and park officials began clearing thousands of tourists and visitors from the site, Okoumou insisted that she would not come down "until all the children are released."

In this brilliant and stirring book, *Unsung America*, Prerna Lal connects Okoumou's demonstration and other more recent protests to the long and still unfolding history of immigrant resistance—one that has for more than a century sought to expose the viciousness of immigration enforcement in the United States while calling for its reformation and imagining a different future for America. Just as the poet Langston Hughes decried this country's "stupid plan [o]f dog eat dog, of mighty crush the weak" while exhorting another ethos also present in America, so too do Lal, Okoumou, and the many others whose visionary stories are introduced in *Unsung America* lay bare the truths of racialized violence in the very foundations of the United States, while giving life to an incipient alternative borne of the struggles of those who resisted slavery, indigenous genocide, and immigrant exclusion.

Unsung America reveals that the shameful and dehumanizing treatment of children at the border are not exceptional but emblematic of the brutality of immigration enforcement and US nation-building since its inception. Through the stories Lal recounts, we learn that the violence manifested in the caging of immigrant children was honed in the separation of millions of other families, with the detention and deportation of mothers, fathers, and siblings over the course of decades. These practices were cultivated earlier still through the incarceration of mostly indigent youth deprived of the second chances afforded to their more affluent peers. And before that, through the internment of the Japanese, the removal of Native American children from their homes and of indigenous peoples from their lands, and in the kidnapping, shackling, and enslavement of Africans to build private wealth in America. Beyond the borders of the

United States, too, Lal's protagonists expose how the imperial quest for exploited labor, land, and political control has wrought immiseration and instability around the world while precipitating new waves of migration to this country. In other words, the most egregious violence, degradation, and hypocrisy involved in contemporary immigration enforcement have long been in practice here—this brutality is not a rare deviation but a defining characteristic of this country's history and its persistent legacies.

Yet, *Unsung America* also holds open the possibility that, as Langston Hughes writes, "America will be!"—that the radically diverse assembly of people on this land, including formerly enslaved people, immigrants from across the globe, and indigenous inhabitants, could come together to create a more just and peaceful world. It is this struggle against US nationalist violence and to make a better world possible that animates the poignant life stories that Prerna Lal lifts up in *Unsung America*.

This struggle for a more just world is manifested most recently in the contemporary movements that understand immigration justice as connected necessarily to the unfinished work of abolition. But Lal makes plain that abolition should be understood not simply as the abolition of the government agency, Immigration and Customs Enforcement (ICE), nor even as the end of immigration enforcement more broadly. Instead, abolition entails working to create a more equitable society, without militarized borders or immigration chokeholds, and with universal access to a dignified, sustainable form of collective life. This is the egalitarian society—open, democratically reconstituted, inclusive—that was the unfulfilled hope of black abolitionists in the nineteenth century and ultimately the unrealized promise of America.

The first stories in *Unsung America* are those of black abolitionists and others who fought the horrors of slavery, and from their struggles we learn that after the end of the Civil War, the dismantling of the institution of slavery was accomplished, at least in part, with the prohibition of chattel slavery, but the positive goal of abolitionists to constitute a new, more equitable social order remained unfulfilled. Untold numbers of black people were lynched or criminalized for minor or nonexistent offenses, and then forced to return to labor on the plantations where they had worked as slaves—a history recorded by W.E.B. DuBois and others. Lal reveals further that among the earliest known deportation plans were efforts to remove emancipated black people from the United States. For example, more than one hundred emancipated black people perished in the course of their removal to the desolate island of Ile-a-Vache in the Caribbean. Lal recognizes a shared struggle for abolition and a more just social order to have commenced with black people who resisted kidnapping, forced migration, brutal unfreedom, and with Native Americans who fought against their forced removal from their lands.

The object of Lal's account, however, is not to claim any likeness between immigration and slavery, or indigenous dispossession and slavery. Instead, this history serves to deepen our understanding that exclusionary and restrictionist immigration measures originate in the institutions of slavery and indigenous genocide, and to recognize the work on the part of African Americans and Native Americans to challenge and expand the meaning of citizenship and to resist exclusionary conceptions of America. Importantly, too, this history shows that the struggles of immigrants, Native Americans, and African Americans may be more closely connected than is sometimes acknowledged.

Unsung America locates a common impulse to justice in the civil disobedience of over ninety thousand Chinese immigrants in the late nineteenth century. Chinese immigrants associated with the Chinese Six Companies organized in the late 1800s to oppose the forced registration of Chinese immigrants, predominantly called the "Dog Tag Law." This massive Chinese American civil disobedience effectively crippled the efforts of the government to surveil and remove Chinese peoples from the United States en masse. We learn as well of the stories of immigrants like John Turner, Emma Goldman, Marcus Garvey, Harry Bridges, Carl Hill, and Prerna Lal (the author) who fought their own deportation cases and while doing so sought to advance their respective ideals of greater freedom in this country, ranging from anarchism to socialism to black economic independence to queer liberation.

These struggles for social, racial, and economic justice continue today in the twenty-first century work of certain immigrants who have organized to advance the proposition that there are millions of people who are Americans in all respects but legally. Lal recounts the stories of the courageous youth who have infiltrated detention centers to organize for the release of incarcerated people there and crashed the border to demand an end to inhumane border restrictionism. The abolitionist struggle for a new beginning in America reverberates as well, we learn, in the solidarities between contemporary movements for immigration justice and racial justice—the call for "Not One More Deportation" that accompanies the Movement for Black Lives demand to "End the War on Black People"; and the dreams of Therese Patricia Okoumou and others—that principles of liberty might one day be realized in a "homeland of the free" leading "all the children to be released."

But how will America become America, how will it move from our vicious and inequitable present to a freer and more just future? Lal offers us the crucial beginnings of an answer by helping us to see and understand more deeply the common bonds that compose already an alternative assembly of peoples. We might think of *Unsung America* as the prehistory of how a better world may come to be. The collective struggles and individual stories Lal lifts up clarify the scope of what we must oppose together and ultimately what we must build. *Unsung America* will leave you transformed and inspired to build this world together.

INTRODUCTION

• • • • • • • • • • •

This is not a book about heroes.

This is a book about courageous people who sometimes made mistakes. People in difficult situations that they often did not choose. People who decided to act despite grave risk and uncertainty. People who were not in the right place at the right time. Through their stories, they tell a history of exclusion, bravery, resilience, and perseverance.

This is a book about immigrant trailblazers. Some passed on after making rich contributions. Many are still alive and continue to battle on for their freedom. The trailblazers in this book are unsung and have been ignored in favor of a narrative that either portrays immigrants as heroes or as villains.

When I was first approached to write a book about awesome immigrants, I thought I was the wrong person for the task, though not because I don't think immigrants are awesome. We definitely are.

Most of us speak multiple languages. We leave our homes and embark on dangerous journeys and come to America seeking freedom and opportunity. We have lost our homes and yet work to create new ones. We have introduced the world to some of their favorite foods—tacos and curry and adobo and kimchi and injera. We create jobs as entrepreneurs, clean homes and office buildings, care for the ill as doctors and nurses, and feed the country through our work in agriculture. We have amazing, complicated names that are hard to pronounce and actually mean something. We make this country the rich, vibrant, diverse, and multicultural place that it is.

A whole encyclopedia could be written about immigrant entrepreneurs or valedictorians. But I did not want to only profile successful immigrants, the ones who made it in the United States. I am tired of that narrative. I am exhausted from how many times I have been asked to play respectability politics, asked to propose a model minority narrative. I have learned the hard way that perfect grades, perfect resumes, and perfect behavior did not prevent us from being the target of legal, political, or immigration enforcement efforts to forcibly remove us from our homes.

After the end of the transatlantic slave trade, American and British industry leaders scoured the world for a cheap source of labor. The British found it in East Indians and brought 60,965 people, including my great-great-grandparents, to the islands of Fiji to work on sugar cane plantations as indentured servants. After indentured servitude ended forty years later, many Indians decided to stay. Although indenture had been brutal, they had lost all semblance of caste, acquired a new language, and built new lives in Fiji. It became home. When the British colonial experiment ended in 1970, the Indian and indigenous population struggled to live in harmony in a post-colonial era.

Fortunately, my grandparents and parents were not born into any kind of servitude, and they were able to build successful lives for themselves in an economy that promised upward mobility. Therefore, it came as a complete shock to my system when my father asked me to pack my bags for the United States in 1999. He had an urgency to move that I could not understand.

I was almost fifteen years old when we came to live in the San Francisco Bay Area. I spent the next decade of my life trying to make sense of where I was and why he had brought me here. Who leaves golden sandy beaches, rich blue lagoons, and emerald-shimmering seas to live in an earthquake zone where it is cold most of the summer? And without a plan to ensure that I could go to college and not spend the rest my life struggling?

Granted, I could have died in Fiji. I was a little queer kid, and I was never good at hiding it. My classmates were mostly Christian zealots. My high school principal would have loved nothing more than to expel me for being gay. And my best gal pal at the time was as powerless as I was to do anything about it, even though we did our best to protect one another. In my father's head, the Bay Area was the only safe place, and many years later, I realized that my parents had made the best choice they could with the information they had at the time.

I took pieces of my home with me—photos of me with my best friends, a Fijian baseball cap, a keychain with a map of the islands, a small desk flag, my favorite tattered green bath towel, and my childhood pillow and blanket.

More vivid than those things, I also carried memories with me. In the weeks before we left, I promised myself that I would imprint in my memory everything about my home, so that it would never be lost to me, and that in my moments of trial, I could use these memories to ground myself, and to seek strength from them. Sometimes I can recall conversations from childhood more easily than the ones I had yesterday.

Immigrants are often told to get in line, and I did. However, a complex tapestry of immigration laws rendered me without status shortly after we arrived in the United States. My US citizen grandmother had filed paperwork to sponsor my mother (and by extension also me as her child) but that paperwork also established that we had intent to immigrate permanently to the United States. Therefore, when I applied for a student visa to continue my studies, the United States government denied it because my grandmother's petition served as evidence that

I had intent to reside here permanently. I was eighteen when I lost status.

As the youngest child and the only one without papers, sending me back to Fiji was not an option for my parents. But it did mean having to live without status in the United States for an indeterminate period.

For a long time, I lived in fear for my life. I was afraid to go to the hospital when I broke my hand, afraid to report violence at home, afraid to ask for help even when I was the victim of a crime, afraid to tell teachers and friends in college that I needed financial support, afraid to apply for jobs or seek scholarships—all out of fear that someone would find out I was undocumented and report me to Immigration and Customs Enforcement (ICE). I feared that I would never be able to graduate from college and live to my full potential.

To pay my way through college and graduate school, I worked as a janitor, cleaning homes and office buildings. When I turned twenty-four, my parents finally received lawful permanent residency (popularly known as "Green Cards"). However, since I was no longer a child, the Obama administration sought to remove me from my home and separate me from my family. By this point, all my family had legal status except for me. My only papers were the couple of degrees under my belt, and I was hungrily trying to get more. I was almost done with law school—as if anyone who wanted me deported ever cared about my academic credentials or achievements.

More importantly, I became a target for removal from the United States because I had become part of a mini-movement of undocumented rabble-rousers who were finished with hiding in the shadows, and instead were organizing to prevent the deportation of thousands of other undocumented people. We blogged, wrote letters, marched, met with politicians, testified before congressional members, occupied buildings and streets, chained ourselves to things, and even infiltrated immigrant detention facilities. Many of these stories are profiled in this book. Many more are likely lost because of a history that marginalizes subaltern voices.

I still clung to half-remembered, half-forgotten memories of Fiji. I never went to a beach, because I feared that it would remind me of all that I had lost. I stopped doing things that I had loved. I stopped living. I did not make any friends. I did not want to form any ties. I did not want to ever love and lose again.

So I devoted myself to accumulating something I would never lose: knowledge. An old Indian parable taught me that knowledge was something that thieves could not steal. In college, Michel Foucault, who ironically was also banned from the United States, taught me that knowledge was power. So when the Notice to Appear for removal proceedings came, I was prepared.

I did not fight deportation because I wanted to. There was nothing I wanted more than to go home. I fought because I would only go home on my own terms. I was going to go back to Fiji with a Green Card in my hand, to sip fresh coconut water from the husk, and enjoy the land's surreal beauty like an American tourist.

It took a historic Supreme Court decision for me to finally gain lawful status. On June 26, 2013, the US Supreme Court struck down the Defense of Marriage Act (DOMA), and my same-sex US citizen partner could finally sponsor me as her spouse. I became a lawful permanent resident on August 1, 2014.

The next week, I found myself in Canada, and two weeks later, I was back in Fiji, catching up on fifteen years of my life.

I was thirty-four when I finally became a United States citizen and voted in my first election. By this time, I had learned to survive without papers as an undocumented, unapologetic, unafraid, queer, and unashamed person. I had also learned that home was not a place, but one that I instead built based on friendships, community, and with my supportive and loving partner.

Now I could go from surviving to thriving. I started living again, opened up my own law practice, and became the parent of a rescue pup, Rosie. She likes to eat, sleep, run, and hopes to one day catch a duck. More than anything, she makes me want to keep things simple, too. I obsess about making sure that she has all her papers, even as I help other immigrants live the same complete life that I am now living.

I share my story only to illustrate how we as immigrants come in all shapes and sizes from all over the world. We have many stories to tell—of escaping persecution in our homelands, of arriving as employees and overstaying our visas, of surviving unscrupulous employers, and terrible immigration attorneys mishandling our cases. And no matter what our status, color, creed, or tongue, we are no less deserving of civil and human rights.

We are drawn to America's promise and protection, and betrayed by its peril. We are part of families who were exiled, siblings who were separated, and grandparents who never knew us. We are sad, angry, scared, but also funny, joyful, and grateful for a second chance at building a new home and life. The stories prove that we, like you, are worth fighting for and fighting over.

In the coming chapters, you will be introduced to many pioneers who fought hard to ensure the freedoms that we take for granted as immigrants. You will learn about the laws that were created just to deport us and about how we have responded. You will learn about our struggle, our mistakes, and our humanity. And hopefully, by the end, you will identify with us as we continue to fight to live where we belong.

THE PROMISE AND PERIL OF CITIZENSHIP

• • • • • • • • • • •

It's a grave oversight to talk about immigration without first focusing on the history of African Americans and Asian Americans. Even before the existence of the United States, the Atlantic Slave Trade separated millions of Africans from their families, forcibly removed them from their homes, and set them on a dangerous journey to the Americas to meet the demand for enslaved labor in the new colonies. Millions died, and millions were forever separated from their homes and loved ones. Even though Africans who were enslaved did not come to this country as immigrants, the history of immigration policy in the United States is inextricably bound up in their experiences and the fight for freedom that they and their descendants undertook.

In the United States, the institution of chattel slavery reduced African persons to property that could be bought and sold by their enslavers. After abolishing chattel slavery, the United States welcomed cheap labor from China to build the transcontinental railroads, and to work in mining and agriculture. Similar labor demands today are filled by immigrants working low-wage jobs, and who also do not have access to citizenship.

Immigration in the United States is a system of exclusion and deportation, and the entire premise comes from policies designed to control and regulate slavery, forcibly remove Native Americans, and later on, exploit the labor of Chinese immigrants. At first, deportation was used to punish behavior deemed wrong or unnatural. As early as 1691, laws provided for the banishment of any white person who married a black person, Native American person, or mixed race person.[1] In the 1700s, enslaved persons were also punished by branding, flogging, and by banishing them from the colony.

Emancipated black people resisted slavery by organizing efforts to free enslaved persons, and because of this, they were also targeted for deportation. As the population of free black people increased, their status became "a foreign element whose social status might not be secure in this country."[2] The earliest known emancipation plans were actually deportation plans, and were published anonymously. A plan for the emancipation of enslaved persons in 1714 also called for the deportation of all black persons who did not want to continue to be enslaved.[3]

Abolitionists and pro-slavery deportation supporters came together to encourage deportations of emancipated and freeborn black persons from the United States. Abolitionists supported the cause because they believed black persons would not integrate and could not live freely in the United States, and pro-slavery deportationists because they wanted to quell slave rebellions and uprisings that were often inspired by the mere existence of free black persons. In this era, even those who opposed deportations wanted to design laws that would make it so difficult for black persons to live freely in the United States that they would leave for other lands on their own.[4] Today, in immigration circles, this policy is called "attrition through enforcement."

Even though the Constitution grants Congress the power to make immigration laws, many colonies, and later states, sought to exercise this power to control their own populations. State legislatures created their own laws to remove free black persons or to ban them from entering the state.[5] Some state laws allowed local law enforcement, such as sheriffs, to remove free black persons if they refused to leave the state willingly. Over time, the deportation of free black persons to other states removed radical black leaders and anti-slavery supporters from the United States. In this way, many states quelled political dissent to slavery, and prevented liberation efforts, such as the Underground Railroad, from becoming full-scale social movements.

As a country, the United States continued to explore deporting former slaves as a solution to the political challenges created by its racist regime. The same president who emancipated slaves also toyed with plans to remove them to maintain the racial pecking order. Even after signing the Emancipation Proclamation, Abraham Lincoln asked the Dutch, British, Haitians, Colombians, and Ecuadorians to take in the emancipated black persons, and he even got Congress to grant him $500,000 to start a colony of free black persons on the desolate island of Île-à-Vache in the Caribbean.[6] But many of these people were removed only to face their deaths: more than 100 of the 450 sent to Île-à-Vache died, and President Lincoln had to send a ship to rescue the survivors.

Free black abolitionists, such as Richard Allen, James Forten, and Robert Purvis, resisted deportation and efforts to send them elsewhere. As the federal government expanded westward through land grabs and gained more power over immigration, Asian immigrants replaced black persons as the unassimilable "others." They faced a new era of exclusionary laws from the states and federal governments. And well into the twentieth century, states continued to forcibly isolate or remove immigrants and black persons via restrictive housing ordinances and public welfare laws.

The stories of free black persons in this chapter are not intended to recast them as immigrants, but to help us understand that policies designed to exclude immigrants have their basis in the institution of slavery, and in the resistance to the institution. I also include them to acknowledge and celebrate the efforts of African Americans in obtaining citizenship and civil rights, which helped later immigrants live more freely. And finally, these stories show that perhaps our struggles are more interconnected than we thought initially. If so, perhaps non-black immigrants today should fight not just for themselves, but alongside and together with black immigrants who continue to experience higher rates of detention and deportation, and black U.S. citizens who continue to be deprived of the full benefits of citizenship and equality under the law.

Dred Scott

The Naturalization Act of 1790 limited citizenship to free white persons of good character.[7] This meant that Native Americans, indentured servants, enslaved persons, free black persons, and anyone else who was not classified as white could not gain citizenship. Thus, the notion of citizenship became central to the struggle for full equality in America. Many African Americans thought that if they could gain citizenship, they would gain freedom, and with it, full civil, economic, and political rights. This may sound eerily familiar, but few literary works focus on the integral role that black Americans played in winning the right to citizenship, and how that struggle helped immigrants.

Born with slave status in Virginia in 1799, in 1846 Dred Scott sued for his freedom and that of his wife and their two daughters, entering into a legal battle that would last eleven years and change the course of history. The basis of the lawsuit was that even though he had been born born with slave status, Dred Scott had lived with his enslaver and US Army commander Dr. John Emerson in states and territories where slavery was illegal, according to both state laws and the Northwest Ordinance of 1787. Legal precedent warranted granting him freedom.

His case eventually made its way to the Supreme Court. In 1857, Chief Justice Roger Taney declared in a 7–2 decision that neither Dred Scott nor any other person of African ancestry could claim citizenship in the United States, and therefore they had no right to even make a claim in court.[8] The decision also noted that Congress did not have the authority to outlaw slavery as it was integral to the United States Constitution.

This decision aroused outrage and deepened existing regional tensions such that after President Abraham Lincoln's Emancipation Proclamation in 1863, the country plunged into a civil war over the economics of slavery and the political control of the country. The Union, representing the Northern states, wanted to keep the United States intact, whereas the Confederates wanted to secede because they believed that the federal government was usurping their authority to exploit labor, skills, and knowledge stolen from enslaved people, and destroying their economies in the process.

With the Confederates losing and finally surrendering in 1865, Congress quickly passed and ratified the Reconstruction Amendments. The Thirteenth Amendment abolished slavery. The Fourteenth granted citizenship to all persons born in the United States, and the Fifteenth gave all men the right to vote.

Of particular importance is the Fourteenth Amendment, which provided citizenship to people who were formerly enslaved, their progeny, and to all persons born in the United States. Besides providing equal rights for citizens, the Fourteenth Amendment provided a basic level of rights to all persons, whether citizens or not. All persons, regardless of immigration status, were to enjoy due process rights with respect to life, liberty, and property, as well as equal protection rights.

Dred Scott never lived to see the Civil War or the enactment of these amendments to the Constitution. On the heels of the unfavorable Supreme Court decision in 1857, he was sold to another family, and was freed by them in 1858. He died from tuberculosis a year after he obtained freedom. However, his fight for citizenship would later help countless immigrants enjoy the benefits that he did not live to enjoy.

German Immigrant Abolitionists

"We hold ourselves as free men who did not escape slavery in our homelands to support it here in America."

—Carl Strehly and Eduard Mühl

In discussions of slavery and civil rights, there is scant mention of immigrants. The majority of the focus on resistance to slavery rightly goes to black freedom fighters, such as Frederick Douglass and Harriet Tubman, who fought slavery by serving as "conductors" of the Underground Railroad. But we also have to highlight how some Anglo-Americans, including the Framers of the United States Constitution, despised slavery and supported abolition. Besides Ella Lonn's pioneering work on how the Irish, German, and other ethnic Americans experienced the Civil War differently from their white counterparts, not much else has been written about immigrants and the role they played in abolishing slavery in the United States.

Benjamin Franklin, one of the Framers of the United States Constitution and an abolitionist, abhorred German immigrants, and wanted controls on their immigration to the

United States. He claimed that they were not smart, didn't adopt local values, and endangered the whiteness of New England.[9] Many German immigrants came from homelands where they did not have full citizenship rights—they could not vote, did not have the right to own property, or were subjected to high taxation and lacked freedom of speech. In the early nineteenth century, some had even fought against despotic rule in the German Confederation, and they moved to the new United States, expecting to share similar ideals.

As newly arrived immigrants with idealistic values, they were distraught when confronted with the institution of slavery. Slavery was an even harsher system of rights deprivation than what they had experienced, and one that contradicted the freedom and democracy that they were expecting in their new home. Some Germans, particularly the ones in Midwestern states, such as Missouri, had a radical idea that posed a special kind of problem to the new republic: they wanted to abolish slavery, and equated anti-slavery with immigrant rights.

These first-generation German immigrants included Friedrich Münch, Carl Strehly, Eduard Mühl, and Arnold Krekel. Together, they served as editors and contributors of German language newspapers in Missouri, writing articles and commentary against slavery in the 1800s, before the rise of popular abolitionist sentiments.

Friedrich Münch, in particular, penned many articles in the 1850s and 1860s in opposition to slavery, and successfully mobilized thousands of Germans to join the Union Army to fight the Confederates in the Civil War. He also opposed deportation of people who were formerly enslaved, stating, "We've no right to send away people who were born here, who have committed no crime, and who have indeed worked for the common good of their neighbors."[10] Yet Münch was no hero; he made decisions that were hypocritical and repugnant despite his advocacy. He purchased an enslaved person to help his wife with chores. He could not foresee integration, and so he proposed resettling emancipated people in a separate territory, such as Florida.

In a similar vein, fellow German journalists, such as Carl Strehly and Eduard Mühl, wrote against slavery in the 1840s for *Hermanner Wochenblat* before it became a popular movement.[11] Initially, they were against abolition of slavery, and thought that the moral arguments against slavery would certainly turn the tide, but they changed their minds as they became disillusioned with the lack of progress.

Unlike the other first-generation German immigrants who came from educated and bourgeoisie backgrounds, Arnold Krekel came to the United States when he was seventeen years old from Prussia and had no fortune.[12] He worked low-wage jobs to support himself as his family settled in St. Charles, Missouri, where Krekel experienced much antagonism from the pro-slavery population. In response to growing nativism against German and Irish immigrants, Krekel founded the *St. Charles Demokrat* in 1852. He was appointed as a US Western District Court judge by Abraham Lincoln, and presided over the Missouri Constitutional Convention of January 11, 1865, signing into law the Ordinance of Emancipation, which freed all the enslaved people in Missouri without any compensation to the enslavers.[13]

These German immigrants were regarded with much scorn where they lived. Their neighbors threatened them with violence and guerilla warfare because of their anti-slavery, pro-Union agenda. They were also living in extremely xenophobic times. The newly arrived Irish and German immigrants found themselves targeted by the nativist Know-Nothing movement.

After the Civil War, many Germans integrated over time with Anglo-Americans and abandoned their support for black liberation, though German immigrant pioneers such as Münch and Krekel continued to support and advance black suffrage and education. In this way, they helped to define a notion of American citizenship that valued racial justice, labor rights, and suffrage for all.

While these early German immigrants were unable to eradicate the negative impacts of slavery, their efforts helped create a more just society. Their conflict with native-born Americans shows us that immigrants did not need to adopt regressive anti-black views. Still, even with some foreign-born allies, it was up to African Americans to lead the struggle that ultimately won citizenship for all persons born in the United States.

Wong Kim Ark

Even after the passage of the Reconstruction Amendments, states still saw it within their authority to invoke police power to control migration at the state level. California tried to limit and exclude Chinese immigrants based on their earlier use of police powers to restrict black migration to the state.[14] After the courts struck down taxation laws designed to target Chinese immigrants, California began to focus on character and conduct, such as lewd behavior, in order to craft laws for restricting Chinese migration. And "as California goes, so goes the nation."

Instead of quelling these discriminatory state laws, the federal government passed exclusionary laws against the Chinese. The Page Act of 1875 prohibited the entry of immigrants who were considered undesirable, including anyone from Asia coming as a contract laborer, any Asian women engaging in prostitution, and any convict from another country.[15]

Unsatisfied with the Page Act, Congress followed up with the 1882 Chinese Exclusion Act, which explicitly placed a ten-year ban on immigrants from China, a clear example of race-based exclusion.[16] The Chinese Exclusion Act of 1882 was amended and renewed several times. Subsequent acts extended the discrimination by prohibiting reentry after leaving the United States, and requiring all existing Chinese residents to obtain a certificate of residency in order to prevent deportation. The Exclusion Act and later reauthorizations banned all legal migration from China, and Chinese immigrants living in the United States were denied citizenship even if born in the United States.

One of the people denied citizenship was Wong Kim Ark, who was born in San Francisco in 1873 to noncitizen parents. When he was twenty-one, he visited his parents, who had returned to China. When Wong Kim Ark returned to the United States in 1895, he was denied entry on the grounds that he was not a United States citizen. Instead, he was confined on board the steamship, and had to file a writ of habeas corpus for his freedom. He was asked to present two white witnesses who could attest to his birth, because as a Chinese person, his own testimony carried no weight in the eyes of the law.

His case made its way to the U.S. Supreme Court, which explicitly rejected limitations on birthright citizenship and ruled that Wong Kim Ark was a United States citizen by virtue of his birth on US soil, even though his parents were not US citizens.[17] The acceptance of birthright citizenship in 1898—a time when hysteria over Chinese immigrants was high—

advanced the fundamental constitutional value of *jus soli* for all. Over time, courts have continued to defeat many efforts to limit birthright citizenship.

Even after he won citizenship, Wong Kim Ark faced persistent discrimination. Whenever he visited his parents abroad and returned to the United States, he was forced to show to show sworn affidavits that he was born in the United States.[18] The United States did not repeal Chinese exclusion policies until 1943.[19]

The federal use of its immigration enforcement power to racially discriminate against Chinese immigrants directly contradicted the Fourteenth Amendment's guarantees of equal protection to all. But despite the ruling in favor of Wong Kim Ark, over the next hundred years, the federal government continued to try to limit the immigration and naturalization of certain ethnic groups. We have these rights today only because people like Dred Scott and Wong Kim Ark stood up to fight for them. And we will only keep these rights if we continue fighting for them.

Chinese Six Companies

With the nation in the grip of hysteria about the supposedly unassimilable Asian immigrants, Congress continued to make new laws targeting them. The Scott Act of 1888 prohibited reentry by Chinese laborers who had left the country. It also nullified all existing certificates of identity that had permitted the bearers to make temporary trips to China.[20]

In 1892, Congress passed the Geary Act, which extended the Chinese Exclusion Act for another ten years, and required Chinese immigrants to register with the US government or face imprisonment with forced labor and deportation.[21] But trying to get a registration certificate (a precursor to the Green Card) most certainly meant forced labor in jail and deportation because most Chinese immigrants at the time were unauthorized migrants who were considered deportable from the United States. It was designed to be a catch-22. No other immigrant group had to carry around documents proving their lawful status until 1928, when the government started issuing immigrant identification cards.[22]

These registration cards had their roots in the system of slavery. Before the Civil War, enslaved people were forced to carry identifying passes when they left the plantation, and free black people were required to bear papers proving that they were not slaves. The new registration requirement fueled anger in the Chinese community, leading to comparisons with "dog tags."

The Geary Act also required white witnesses to testify to a Chinese person's immigration status, and punished unauthorized immigration with one year of imprisonment and hard labor, along with deportation. In an early act of collective civil disobedience, led by the Chinese Six Companies, Chinese refused to register because they considered the law discriminatory and dehumanizing.

Established in 1862, the Chinese Consolidated Benevolent Association (CCBA), also known as the Chinese Six Companies, was an association of Chinese merchants. The main goal of the CCBA was to help Chinese migrants come to the United States and return to China, to take care of poverty-stricken or sick Chinese, and to send their dead back to China for burial.

As the Chinese population grew in the United States and they faced more discrimination, the CCBA got more politically involved. The Six Companies hired lawyers to litigate against discriminatory laws, hired personnel to protect Chinese businesses, campaigned for higher wages and fewer hours for Chinese workers, and smuggled thousands of Chinese across the US-Mexico border between 1882 and 1930.[23]

The Chinese Six Companies led the fight against the Geary Act by posting flyers in Chinatowns urging the 110,000 Chinese in the United States not to register for the "Dog Tag Law." The Six Companies also raised funds to finance litigation against the Geary Act. The campaign was enormously successful and became the largest organized act of civil disobedience in United

States history. Over 93,445 Chinese didn't register, thereby risking arrest and detention.[24]

The Chinese Six Companies filed a lawsuit to challenge the Geary Act on the basis that hard labor and deportation constituted cruel and unusual punishment under the Eighth Amendment. They also argued that the law violated the Fifth and Sixth Amendments by imprisoning people to do hard labor without trial. Unfortunately, the Supreme Court disagreed and ruled that as a sovereign nation, the United States could choose to detain and deport any person or race.[25] This provided the legal justification for the immigrant detention and deportation regime that exists today.

While the courts upheld the detention and deportation of undocumented Chinese under the Geary Act, the federal government soon realized that it did not have the enforcement capacity to arrest, detain, and deport about 100,000 undocumented Chinese immigrants. Though they did not win in court, the Chinese Six Companies won through civil disobedience, by encouraging people not to register. Therefore, the Geary Act became an unfunded mandate. Over time, the Chinese Six Companies filed lawsuits to carve out and broaden exceptions to the Geary Act for Chinese merchants, students, and family members of Chinese Americans. Congress finally removed these restrictions in 1943, during World War II, in a diplomatic gesture towards its ally, China. However, the remaining restrictions provided the structural basis for detentions and deportations that continue to this day.

Beyond the system of detention and deportation of undocumented migrants, the registration cards and requirements imposed by the Geary Act have carried over into present times. Present-day immigration laws still require immigrants to register with the United States government and inform the government within ten days after moving to a new address. Lawful permanent residents must carry an unexpired registration certificate, popularly known as a Green Card. These cards must be renewed every ten years, even though the permanent resident status itself does not expire. Even today we challenge "show me your papers" laws in states, such as Arizona and Alabama, mandates which the federal government has had on the books for generations.

Kaoru Yamataya

By the early 1900s, the United States had established the power to detain and deport all noncitizens, even without a trial. Deportation served as a social filter by restricting eligibility for citizenship and fundamentally shaping the social composition of the United States. The government enacted provisions to exclude entry to individuals who were poor, involved in sex work, or likely to become a public charge (dependent on the government for assistance). These provisions were primarily used to deny agency to immigrant women as independent economic actors. Individuals were deportable if they were deemed to become a public charge within three years of their entry.

Fifteen-year-old Kaoru Yamataya sought entry into the United States on July 11, 1901, in Seattle, Washington.[26] She was allowed to land, but was arrested four days later, along with her fellow traveler, Masataro Yamataya, who was most likely her trafficker. Ten days after her arrest, immigration officials convened in a hearing presided over by non-judges, in English, a language that Yamataya did not understand. Board of Special Inquiry found that she was a person likely to become a public charge, which meant that she could be deported. They probably made this judgment because Yamataya was visibly pregnant at the time and did not seem to be married or to have relatives in the United States.

At this time in immigration history, targeting women was commonplace. The growing concern over premarital sex, single motherhood, and what was deemed to be inappropriate sexual behavior helped to shape immigration policies that would disproportionately exclude and deport immigrants who were women or girls.[27] Unwed mothers faced deportation, because in this era pregnancy and morality were issues that seemed relevant to good citizenship. Women who were pregnant or suspected of participating in prostitution were the most likely to be deported. Women who arrived at US ports of entry without partners were suspected of coming for immoral purposes, such as engaging in sex work.

The Board of Special Inquiry decided that Yamataya should remain in custody while they requested an order of deportation from the Secretary of the Treasury, which was in charge of immigration enforcement at the time. The Board intended to return her to Japan at the expense of the vessel that had brought her to the U.S. Two months after her arrival, Yamataya gave birth to a baby boy. Unfortunately, he passed away from pneumonia while still in immigration custody.

But Yamataya hired legal counsel and fought back. She contended that she came to the United States to further her education, and that she did not engage in sex work.[28] Yamataya's lawyers contended that she was entitled to due process as someone on US soil, and that the law used by the Board to order her deportation was unconstitutional because it did not provide her with a proper hearing. Due process generally requires notice of allegations, the opportunity to be heard by a judicial officer, and a trial for certain types of judicial proceedings. Technically, Yamataya never received proper due process because non-judicial officials had presided over the hearing, and because it had been conducted in a language she did not understand.

The US Supreme Court decided that the hearing the Board of Special Inquiry had given her was sufficient and ordered Yamataya deported. However, in doing so, the Court ruled that the government could not deport a noncitizen without affording them procedural due process protections, including the right to a hearing. In so doing, the Court clarified that individuals have a right to a hearing even if they enter the country unlawfully and do not establish long-term residence.

Yamataya v. Fisher established the concept of due process for noncitizens, and the decision opened the door for noncitizens to appeal procedural irregularities in their deportation hearings. While this did not help Yamataya, her refusal to accept the questionable actions of men regarding her body and autonomy helped establish a baseline for granting due process to millions of people. Even though deportation is primarily enacted as a punishment, immigrants facing removal are subjected to similar administrative law procedures, which are quite limited in nature. Immigration courts are kangaroo courts, because they are under the purview of the politically motivated Department of Justice, therefore the autonomy and authority of the so-called "immigration judges" is quite questionable.

Yamataya was likely a survivor of sexual violence, at a time when the United States did not have laws that could qualify her for immigration status as a victim of violence. The government's lack of concern about her likely exposure to sexual violence parallels the current lack of concern for Central American women seeking asylum at the US-Mexico border. If caught by Customs and Border Protection (CBP) agents, migrant women are often deported to Mexico's violent border towns in the middle of the night.[29] Rape along the US-Mexico border is so common that it is reluctantly accepted as a potential part of the price for admission to America, and many migrant women take birth control pills before making the dangerous journey north.[30]

The "likely to become a public charge" grounds under which Yamataya was deported continues to shape federal and state immigration policy. The 1996 Personal Responsibility and Work Opportunity Act, and the Illegal Immigration Reform and Immigrant Responsibility Act, eliminated access for lawful permanent residents to many social welfare benefits, such as Medicare, Medicaid, Supplemental Social Security Income, and food stamps.[31] Some of the harsh provisions were later removed after protests from advocates, but confusion about access to benefits is so widespread in immigrant communities, that contrary to popular perception, most forgo receiving any form of assistance. In this manner, poverty is still used as a device to marginalize, if not outright exclude people who are perceived unfit for citizenship.

Bhagat Singh Thind and Takao Ozawa

Even though the Fourteenth Amendment made citizens of all persons born in the United States, Congress still limited citizenship acquired through naturalization to white persons and, through an amendment, added those with African origins.[32] In 1917, Congress specifically banned all Asian persons from immigrating to the United States. Asian Americans were caught in limbo and condemned to second-class status, even those here legally.

Since the process of naturalization at that time was a judicial function, it was up to individual judges to decide who was a white person, or a person of African nativity or African descent. This led to an interesting patchwork of court decisions whereby Iranians and Armenians were able to win naturalization, but Asian Indians and Japanese individuals were deemed to be non-white.[33] Since Asians were excluded until the 1940s, courts heard many cases involving their naturalization. In nearly all of these cases, the applicants claimed whiteness.

One of these seminal cases involved a Japanese immigrant. Takao Ozawa was born in Japan but moved to the United States in 1894, when he was nineteen years old, and grew up in California. He graduated from Berkeley High School, studied at the University of California, Berkeley, and then moved to Hawai'i. He sought naturalization in 1914 and fought his way up to the Supreme Court. In a brief that he wrote to the Court, Ozawa disavowed any connection with Japanese churches, schools, or organizations.[34] He described how he had been educated in the United States. He claimed to speak mostly English and told the court that his children did not speak Japanese at home.

> **"In name, I am not an American, but at heart I am a true American."**
>
> —Takao Ozawa

Ozawa essentially distanced himself from anything having to do with Japan and aimed to present himself higher on the racial pecking order based on his literal and metaphorical whiteness. He conflated being white with being American. Neither the Hawai'i District Court nor the US Supreme Court agreed with him.[35] The United States contended that the proper distinction wasn't based on nativity or skin color, but that "white" was equivalent to European, and none of Ozawa's ancestors had been European.

The Ozawa decision served as precedent until Congress removed barriers for Japanese naturalization in 1952. By the time Ozawa died in 1936, he had made Hawai'i his home, although the United States had failed to consider him as one of its own.

Another major case involved Bhagat Singh Thind (1892–1967), who was born in Punjab, India and came to the United States in 1913. A wave of immigrants came from India at the turn of the century, and by 1910 there were between five and ten thousand Asian Indians in the United States. At the time, anthropologists generally regarded Asian Indians as Caucasian, not Mongolian. In 1918, Thind was actually granted citizenship, only for the document to be voided by the Immigration and Naturalization Service four days later. He served in World War I for the United States, and was honorably discharged, after which he once again applied for United States citizenship while residing in Washington State.

Once again, in 1920, Thind received citizenship, which the government appealed once more, despite his military service to the country. In 1923, the US Supreme Court heard his case. In contrast to Ozawa, Bhagat Singh Thind claimed that as an Asian Indian, he was Caucasian, and therefore white, particularly because of his high caste.As a matter of fact, Aryans had previously colonized India, so Thind based his claim on this history.

The Supreme Court disagreed with him, and ruled that Asian Indians were not eligible for US citizenship. (Even though Thind was Sikh, not Hindu, the courts used the term

'Hindoo' to describe all Asian Indians regardless of religion.)[36] Unfortunately, more than sixty-five Asian Indians were denaturalized in the wake of Thind's case, including A. K. Mozumdar, who had been the first Asian Indian to become naturalized as a white person in 1913.[37]

After the decision, Thind moved to New York, where he again applied for citizenship after Congress passed a law in 1935 that allowed US veterans to become naturalized. After three attempts, Thind finally gained citizenship in 1936 without a challenge from the government.

Thind went on to complete his doctorate degree in the United States, wrote riveting books on Sikh philosophy, and delivered lectures on metaphysics. He campaigned actively for the independence of India from Britain and helped Indian students in any way he could.

Thind and Ozawa tried to prove they were white. They tried to show they had assimilated and that they were deserving of American citizenship. The courts, engaged in trying to legally define the legal construction of race, failed Thind, Ozawa, and many others. Perhaps they would have had more success if they had challenged race-based naturalization laws as being per se inconsistent with the United States Constitution. But we will truly never know.

As history rolled on, undocumented immigrants would try to show that they deserved citizenship because they were Americans in every sense but their papers. They would also fail for at least two decades.

Kajiro Oyama

"I was aware that my rights were being violated but if that's what the president wanted us to do—then we must evacuate. It was my intention to prove my loyalty and looked forward to joining the service. That is—until the property was escheated. My desire to join the service was to defend my country and, more specifically, to defend my home. When they took our home, I changed my attitude completely. I could never be hostile to the USA, but I was bitterly disappointed and felt like a man without a country."

—Fred Yoshihiro Oyama, US citizen, son of Kajiro Oyama

During Oyama's journey to justice, the United States remained opposed to the large number of Asian immigrants arriving through Mexico, Canada, Hawai'i, and even the Philippines, which at the time was a US territory. Individual states could no longer enact immigration laws explicitly excluding people because the Fourteenth Amendment forbade it, so started to focus on creating "facially neutral" property laws that would dissuade the new immigrants from settling in the state. One example was California's Alien Land Law of 1913 (also known as the Webb-Haney Act), which was specifically a response to the thousands of Japanese immigrant farmers who were perceived to be competing with their Anglo-American counterparts. It barred Japanese and other Asian immigrants who were "ineligible to citizenship" from owning agricultural property.[38]

Similar to the Chinese, early Japanese immigrants encountered discrimination in various aspects of their life. On the federal level, the government started to ban their entry into the country in 1907. On the state level, they were prevented from owning property, and schools started to segregate the children of Japanese immigrants.[39] Initially, Japanese immigrants tried to bypass the land laws by purchasing the land in the name of their minor children who were US citizens. Then they could manage the land as the guardians of their childrens' estate. In response to this tactic, in 1920 California amended the Alien Land Law to make anyone who was ineligible for naturalization also ineligible to serve as guardians to property owners. Furthermore, it specified that the purchase of property in the name of someone else would be presumed to represent an attempt to bypass the Alien Land Law and thereby subject to forfeiture.[40]

Over time, other states established anti-Japanese land laws, which for the most part were rarely enforced. But during World War II, after the United States rounded up thousands of Japanese and placed them in internment camps, California funded lawsuits to challenge their property ownership.[41] The goal of the lawsuits were to show hostility toward the Japanese, extort them into selling their property to the state at less than full value, and dissuade them from returning to California.

With the help of the Japanese American Citizens League (JACL), in 1945, Kajiro and Fred Oyama challenged the Alien Land Law.[42] Born in Japan in 1899, Kajiro Oyama came to the United States in 1914 hoping to study at California Institute of Technology.[43] He was ineligible for United States citizenship because, at that time, the process of becoming a naturalized citizen was closed to Japanese individuals on racial grounds. Therefore, because of the Alien Land Law, he also could not own land, so he worked on farms that were leased by his uncle.

In 1923, Oyama bought twenty-three acres in Chula Vista, near San Diego, California, and deeded the property to a white acquaintance, Arthur Glower. Over time, Oyama's farm prospered. He married and established a family in the United States. In 1934, Kajiro Oyama purchased land in San Diego in the name of Fred Oyama, his son, and served as the guardian of the person and estate of his son.[44]

Seven years later, on February 19, 1942, President Roosevelt issued Executive Order 9066, requiring the internment of persons of Japanese ancestry along the West Coast. Kajiro did not want to be placed in an internment camp, so he leased some farmland in Utah, and moved there with four other families during the brief period allowed for "voluntary evacuation."

Although the Oyama family escaped to Utah, California claimed that the purchase of Kajiro Oyama's property had involved a fraudulent evasion of the Alien Land Law, and that the property consequently now belonged to the state of California.

The Oyamas took this case all the way to the US Supreme Court though they changed their tactics along the way. Instead of arguing that the Alien Land Law was a violation of equal protection for both the immigrant parent and the US citizen child, the case focused on the US citizen child and how he was being deprived of property rights.

In 1948, the United States Supreme Court ruled that the Alien Land Law violated Fred Oyama's equal protection rights as a United States citizen.[45] The state of California's attempted confiscation of Fred Oyama's property because of his father's ancestry constituted discrimination based on national origin and race.

At a time when racial discrimination and hostility against the Japanese was at an all-time high, the Oyama family used the legal system to fight for their rights, and for the rights of countless others. The Oyama case helped to turn the tide against the discrimination that continued to be directed recently interned Japanese families. The Oyama case also led to the invalidation of a similar alien land law in Oregon. However, the case missed a critical opportunity to invalidate the racially discriminatory treatment of noncitizens, because it opted to not address the equal protection claim made earlier by Kajiro Oyama, the noncitizen father. This demonstrates the troubling consequences of relying on citizenship as a basis for rights. In so doing, the Supreme Court allowed California to continue to deny land ownership to noncitizens.

The Oyama family never returned to Chula Vista and remained in Utah until 1946.[46] Kajiro Oyama eventually owned and farmed three hundred acres in San Diego County and became a US citizen. He died in 1998, when he was ninety-nine years old.

The California Supreme Court finally, in 1953, declared the Alien Land Law unconstitutional in a test case led by another Japanese immigrant, Sei Fuji,[47] but California did not repeal the law until 1956. In 1988, Congress finally offered an official apology and individual payments of twenty thousand dollars to Japanese Americans who had been held in internment camps during World War II without charges or trial.[48] However, thousands of Japanese immigrants and Japanese American citizens never received the full value of their land nor compensation for the freedoms they had lost.

Claudia Jones

> **"The Lady with the Lamp, the Statue of Liberty, stands in New York Harbor. Her back is squarely turned on the USA. It's no wonder, considering what she would have to look upon. She would weep, if she had to face this way."**
>
> —Claudia Jones

The 1952 McCarran-Walter Act finally lifted racial restrictions on citizenship.[49] However, it added many more barriers as well, including but not limited to deportation for criminal conviction, drug trafficking, homosexuality, prostitution, sexual deviance, crimes of moral turpitude, economic dependency, and polygamy. Yet deportations under these new restrictions did not go unchallenged by advocates, who continued to try to carve out exceptions in the law.

Born Claudia Vera Cumberbatch, Claudia Jones is a classic case of an advocate who challenged her politically motivated deportation. She was born in Trinidad in 1915.[50] When she was about nine years old, her middle-class parents moved to the United States to pursue better opportunities. A few years later, when her parents experienced discrimination during the Great Depression, Jones started to learn about the Jim Crow oppression that black people suffered in America. At seventeen, Jones contracted tuberculosis, which became a lifelong chronic condition, perhaps contributing to her early death.

In 1936, inspired by how the Communist Party had established the public defender system, Jones joined the Young Communist League (YCL). She quickly rose through the ranks, writing many letters and publications to promote black nationalism among the Marxist ranks. As a black nationalist and communist, Jones put black women at the forefront of class struggle. Jones is part of a long tradition of black American women who regarded their oppression as unique from other women and from black men. She popularized the term "triple oppression" to describe black women's oppression and articulated a socialist feminism that considered not just race, but the various struggles of all working women.

Jones was arrested multiple times in violation of the McCarran Act and the Smith Act, laws that limited communist activity, and deported radicals from the United States.[51] Due to her membership in the Communist Party, she could not become a

United States citizen. In the midst of her legal struggles against deportation, Jones suffered heart failure and was hospitalized several times for treatment of coronary heart disease and hypertension. In 1955, Jones was detained for nine months while awaiting deportation. While detained, her colleagues petitioned successfully for her release based on her health. Her colleagues also tried to delay her deportation by requesting a stay because of her health.[52]

Claudia Jones was not deported. Due to her radical views, Great Britain did not want her in Trinidad, which was still a British colony. But because of her influence, they instead offered Jones citizenship in Great Britain.[53] She took the offer and left for Britain in 1955. Jones became an even more popular figure in Britain, contributing to the rise of the British Communist Party. Scholars believe that Jones was to the left of Karl Marx, because Jones believed that capitalism alone did not account for racism and sexism. Ironically, Jones is buried to the left of Karl Marx in London's Highgate Cemetery.[54]

Claudia Jones challenged the idea of citizenship and belonging being based solely on the circumstance of her birth. She was brought here as a child and raised in the United States. Her political work is what caused her deportation, because the United States considered radical thought to be threatening and inherently foreign, even though Jones was as American as one could be.

Jones referred to her deportation as an exile, pointing out that instead of being forced to go back to her origin, she was being banished.[55] In due course, long-term residents, people brought here as children, and people with family ties in the United States, would challenge deportation by adopting a similar language to evoke the pathos of exile.

As we will explore more in the next chapter, immigration enforcement continues to be predicated on excluding those who are deemed a threat or perceived as unfit for US citizenship. The United States continues to deny citizenship to people who have ever been associated with the Communist Party.[56]

Celestino Almeda and the Filipino War Veterans

Before World War II, Asian Americans were an explicit object of racial discrimination under immigration law, which declared all new Asian arrivals as ineligible for US citizenship. But during World War II, Congress granted enlistees the right to naturalize, regardless of their national origin or manner of entry. Until the war ended, this gave all immigrants an incentive to serve and a way for them to naturalize. Between 1943 and 1946, the United States sent naturalization officers from post to post throughout England, Iceland, North Africa, and the Pacific, naturalizing thousands of foreign nationals who were serving with the United States.

Since the United States was in control of the Philippines when the Japanese army invaded the country in 1941, President Franklin Delano Roosevelt signed a presidential order to bring all military forces in the Philippines under US control and as an incentive, allowed Filipino enlistees to become United States citizens if they filed applications by the end of 1946.[57] Before and during the war, Filipinos were considered American nationals, similar to the designation afforded to American Samoans today. At least 250,000 Filipinos answered the call to serve and fought with American forces in World War II against Japanese forces. After the war, in 1946, the Treaty of Manila relinquished US sovereignty, and declared the Philippines an independent nation even while retaining military bases on the island. Fearful that thousands of Filipino veterans would now be eligible for the benefits promised to them during the war, the United States stripped recognition from Filipino soldiers through the Rescission Act of 1946, and it explicitly barred these war veterans from rights, privileges, or benefits. As the cherry on top, the United States also removed a stationed naturalization officer in the Philippines before the war was over, depriving many enlistees the opportunity to even apply to become citizens of the United States.[58]

World War II compelled the United States to ease citizenship barriers; the country came face to face with its hypocrisy as it fought a war against Nazis abroad while openly discriminating against racial and ethnic groups at home. Congress abolished naturalization quotas with regard to Chinese in 1943, Indians, and Filipinos in 1946, and Japanese and all others, regardless of nationality in 1952.[59] Finally, in 1965, Congress eliminated racial quotas in immigration law, and opened the door to immigration based on family and employment.[60] The changes allowed new Filipino immigrants to come to the United States, and reinvigorated the desire to emigrate to the US among Filipino veterans, who were now middle-aged.

After almost twenty years, Filipino veterans finally began their struggle to recapture the immigration and military benefits that were denied them at the end of World War II. The first veteran to challenge the denial was Marciano Haw Hibi.

Born in Manila in 1917, Hibi enlisted in the Philippines Scouts, a United States Army unit, in 1941.[61] He was captured by Japanese soldiers and released after six months of internment. In April 1945, after the liberation of the Philippines, Hibi rejoined the Scouts and served until his honorable discharge in December 1945. Hibi entered the United States in 1964 on a visitor-for-business visa and filed for naturalization. He asserted that even though he served in the war, the United States failed to inform him of his right to naturalize in due time, and this amounted to affirmative misconduct. In 1967 the district court agreed with Hibi, and the Ninth Circuit upheld the decision, but the Supreme Court dismissed his case on appeal in 1973.[62]

Inspired by Hibi, other Filipino war veterans filed similar lawsuits—individually and in class actions, alleging that the United States had acted in bad faith in 1945 by removing the only naturalization officer in the Philippines, to ensure that veterans would not be able to naturalize in time.[63] They ultimately lost the class action, but their plight reached the ears of some in Congress. In 1990, President George H.W. Bush signed a law offering citizenship to all Filipino war veterans still alive.[64] In this manner, some Filipino war veterans finally became United States citizens, but about fifty years late.

However, even with United States citizenship, the struggle of these veterans continued. Many who immigrated died without reuniting with their sons and daughters, because the sponsorship process to bring them from the Philippines took so long. Of the 4,500 still alive, many were denied benefits under the law.

One example was Celestino Almeda. Before World War II he was a vocational industrial arts instructor in a high school in the Philippines. In 1941 he answered President Roosevelt's call and enrolled in active duty with the Anti-Sabotage Regiment[65] of the US Philippine Commonwealth Army Forces.[66] He was honorably discharged in 1946 and kept meticulous records of his service. Almeda finally became a US citizen in 1996. However, since many records had been destroyed or erased, his name was not in the Army's National Personnel Records, so despite having gained citizenship, he was denied veteran benefits and recognition for his service.

In 2009, the Obama administration provided one-time payments: $15,000 for US citizens and $9,000 for Filipino citizens.[67] By the end of 2017, $226 million had been awarded to more than twenty-two thousand people. But Department of Veterans Affairs records also show that more than half of the applicants who tried to qualify were denied. Until recently, Almeda was one of them.

Almeda represented the American Coalition for Filipino Veterans as a spokesperson and testified before Congress.[68] A resident of Gaithersburg, Maryland, Almeda became a regular feature in the hallways of congressional buildings. He spoke to as many legislators as he could about the plight of war veterans such as himself who had served honorably but had been cast aside. In 2017, at the age of one hundred, Almeda finally received $15,000 from the Department of Veteran Affairs.[69] He also received a Congressional Gold Medal—the highest civilian honor bestowed by Congress—and many salutes from members of Congress.[70]

Alas, many thousands died awaiting the day the United States would recognize their service. Regardless of what one may think of military service, the United States foreclosed a path to citizenship, rescinded veteran's benefits, and denied recognition to Filipino war veterans for their brave wartime service. Even today, immigrants who have served in the United States military are denied recognition, face deportation for decades-old convictions, and have to worry about family members being deported. They deserve better.

Lundy Khoy

One and a half million refugees from Cambodia, Vietnam, and Laos came to the United States as refugees during the 1980s. Their children were very young and grew up as Americans. As refugees in the United States, they faced many obstacles, including language barriers, being resettled in neighborhoods with high crime and unemployment rates, and mental health needs stemming from war-related trauma.

Adjustment was particularly difficult for Cambodian refugees who fled a genocide that killed one third of the population. Ninety-nine percent of Cambodian refugees had faced starvation, ninety percent had lost a close relative in the genocide, and seventy percent continued to suffer from depression.[71] Faced with these difficulties, many of the younger refugees who grew up in the United States turned to gangs as surrogate families, and to drugs for escapism.

Lundy Khoy was born in a Thai refugee camp to Cambodian parents who fled the war that had torn their country apart. When Khoy was just one year old, her family was resettled in the United States. When she was nineteen, Khoy fell in with a bad crowd. After a night of partying, a police officer asked her if she had any drugs. She truthfully said she had several tabs of ecstasy, resulting in her arrest for possession with intent to distribute.[72] Khoy pled guilty and was given a five-year sentence in criminal court. She was detained by ICE officers, and informed that she would be deported to Cambodia.

Since Cambodia did not issue the travel documents necessary for deportation, Khoy was eventually released from detention. She returned home, finished school, went back to work, actively volunteered in multiple charities in her community, and eventually got married and had a son with her US citizen husband. After working with a filmmaker to document her story in the short film, *Save Lundy*, she began to advocate in Congress for fair and humane deportation laws. In 2016, Khoy was granted a Governor's pardon.

Unfortunately, Southeast Asians such as Khoy are three to four times more likely to be deported for old criminal convictions than people from other migrant communities.[73] Since 1998, over fifteen thousand individuals have received final orders of deportation to Cambodia, Laos, and Vietnam.[74] Through her advocacy, Khoy changed what could have been a disaster, but thousands more have not been given a second chance. They are sent back to countries where they have never set foot before, since many were born in refugee camps outside their parents' countries of origin.

Over time, naturalization became the government's second line of defense against immigrants they considered undesirable. Nowadays, immigrants are thoroughly vetted before they can gain lawful permanent residence. And they are vetted again when they apply for US citizenship. In this manner, all immigrants are vetted at least twice before they can become citizens.

The current deportation regime has its roots in efforts to exclude African Americans and Asian Americans. But ironically, these groups remain at the periphery of the debate over immigration policies and reforms. Though today, deportations do not just target black and Asian immigrants, the deportation regime continues to be racialized, even as the government increasingly uses the criminal justice system to funnel people into the prison-deportation pipeline.[75]. Black immigrants still are disproportionately targeted for deportations, as are Southeast Asian refugees like Khoy.[76]

Nothing compares to the Fugitive Slave Acts that treated black persons as equivalent to property. But the laws that allowed local authorities to pursue free black persons and fugitives from slavery now emulated by state law enforcement to arrest, detain, and deport immigrants. Engineered by modern-day white nationalists, states such as Arizona, Georgia, Florida, and Alabama have passed brutal laws against undocumented immigrants for the purpose of "attrition through enforcement." These laws do not just harm immigrants. Because of the racialized regime of enforcement, they also target United States citizens, many of whom have been arrested, detained, and deported.

In order to cut through the current impasse on immigration, immigrant rights, and criminal justice, the political struggles of brown and black people and others need to recognize our shared experiences and common goals, so that we can together build a racial justice movement. Without actively working and building alliances in black communities, non-black immigrant rights advocates risk isolating ourselves from those with whom we have the most in common.

DEPORTING DISSENT

• • • • • • • • • • •

Under the Trump administration, the United States expand
to Immigration and Customs Enforcement (ICE) has detained
or deported several prominent immigrant activists across
the country.

In Jackson, Mississippi, ICE arrested and detained Daniela
Vargas, an undocumented immigrant, after she spoke out
about immigration issues at a conference.[77] In Vermont, around
the same time, ICE detained José Enrique Balcazar Sánchez,
Zully Victoria Palacios Rodríguez, Yesenia Hernández-Ramos,
and Esau Peche-Ventura—four organizers with Migrant
Justice, a workers' rights organization.[78] In Tucson, Arizona,
a federal judge ordered the deportation of Alejandra Pablos,
a well-known immigration and reproductive rights activist,
after denying her case for asylum.[79] In Seattle, Washington,
Maru Mora-Villalpando, an activist who heads the Northwest
Detention Center Resistance (NWDCR), received a Notice
to Appear in removal proceedings because of her continued
resistance to the deportation regime.[80] These cases are not
unique. Indeed, federal lawsuits document over twenty cases of
undocumented immigrant activists arrested nationwide in the
last couple years.[81]

News of these arrests and detentions of migrant activists sent shockwaves through immigrant communities, even though ICE publicly denied targeting them for their political activities.[82] Noncitizens with some level of protection, such as the Deferred Action for Childhood Arrivals (DACA), no longer felt safe, let alone those who have no protection from deportation. But in almost every instance, people visited their loved ones, shared the news on social media, scrambled for legal assistance, and made calls to authorities requesting them to free the advocate facing deportation. Advocates urged people not to let their immigration status lapse, and to not speak out publicly about their immigration statuses. However, putting the onus on those who have taken great risks to advance their cause hardly seems like an adequate answer to the Trump administration's continued assault on immigrant rights.

Deportation as a form of silencing political dissent is hardly a new tactic of the nation state. Donald Trump is making headlines for his proposals to impose ideological tests on immigrants, but the fear of foreigners and their political ideologies has defined US immigration laws for generations.

The United States has long used the threat of deportation as a tool of political control. The horrific assassination of President William McKinley in 1901 at the hands of a self-proclaimed anarchist, Leon Czolgosz, set the stage for congressional action to curb immigration based on ideology alone.[83] Even though Leon Czolgosz was born in the United States, people presumed he was an immigrant because of his surname, triggering a legislative overreaction with the goal of stopping foreign-born anarchists from coming to the United States. Congress responded with the Alien Immigration Act of 1903 ("Alien Act") permitting the exclusion of "...anarchists, or persons who believe in or advocate the overthrow by force or violence of the Government of the United States or of all government or of all forms of law, or the assassination of public officials."[84] But the law was not about national security or taking action against those who threatened public safety. Rather, the new law reflected broader concerns about social and progressive movements that threatened the status quo of United States politics.

For years to come, under the guise of national security and public safety, the US government would use deportation as a way to target political activists, from John Turner, Emma Goldman, and Marcus Garvey, to Tam Tran and other contemporary immigrant rights leaders.

The past and present efforts of the United States government to detain and deport noncitizens base their legitimacy on claims that their targets lack lawful status or are threats to the security of the United States. But as we take a closer look in this chapter, we'll find that at the core of these efforts is an attempt to take away the rights of people who were not born in the United States, including the right to freedom of speech and to organize for social change.

John Turner

Between 1904 and 1916, twenty anarchists were excluded and deported under the new Alien Act.[85] The first one was John Turner.

> **"If no work was being done, if it were Sunday for a week or a fortnight, life in New York would be impossible, and the workers, gaining audacity, would refuse to recognize the authority of their employers and eventually take to themselves the handling of the industries... All over Europe they are preparing for a general strike, which will spread over the entire industrial world. Everywhere the employers are organizing, and to me, at any rate, as an anarchist, as one who believes that the people should emancipate themselves, I look forward to this struggle as an opportunity for the workers to assert the power that is really theirs."**

> —John Turner, excerpt from speech that led to Turner's Deportation

John Turner was an English trade unionist and a philosophical anarchist. He visited the United States in 1896 and lectured extensively on the rights of workers.[86] He then returned in

October 1903, purportedly through Canada instead of Ellis Island, though he never revealed how exactly he entered the United States. Immigration agents arrested him after one of his political speeches and sent Turner to Ellis Island for detention pending deportation.[87] Under questioning at Ellis Island, Turner admitted that he was an anarchist, at which point immigration officials informed him that under the 1903 Immigration Act, he would be deported from the United States. The Free Speech League (a predecessor of the American Civil Liberties Union), an organization at the turn of the last century that focused on combating government censorship, rushed to his aid.[88]

Pending his forced deportation, Turner was allowed to voluntarily leave the United States and return to England, but US anarchist leaders, such as Emma Goldman, asked him to remain in detention on Ellis Island so that they could challenge the constitutionality of his deportation and the constitutionality of the Immigration Act itself, which seemed to encroach on the First Amendment. Turner agreed to endure the indignity of detention in order to fight for his values.

The Free Speech League argued that Turner was a nonviolent, philosophical anarchist, who posed no threat to the United States or its residents. Deporting him for his beliefs would violate the First Amendment's protection of free expression. Lawyers for the United States argued that as a foreigner,

Turner had no First Amendment rights, and that he should be deported in the interest of self-preservation.

Overnight, Turner became a celebrity for a cause that brought together immigrants, trade unionists, and free speech advocates. Protesters filled Cooper Union in New York to object to Turner's deportation. But the Supreme Court agreed with the US government and affirmed his deportation.[89] In doing so, the Court upheld the Alien Act's constitutionality, deferring to Congress's plenary power to exclude foreigners as it wished, and declaring that foreigners held no rights under the US Constitution.

The use of immigration law to effectively punish radicalism reflects the frustration felt by many policymakers of the time that criminal laws were incapable of quashing community organizing. Anarchists and those deemed anarchists by mere affiliation could not be prosecuted criminally for their beliefs, so to assert political and social control, the government inserted anti-radical clauses in the law through the Immigration Act of 1903, which the US Supreme Court upheld as part of the powers granted to Congress.

Over a hundred years after the Turner case, the United States government has continued to claim that people who are not legally admitted to the United States do not have First Amendment rights.[90] When a group of Central American mothers protested their continued detention by launching a hunger strike at Karnes in 2014, ICE officials responded by threatening to take their children away, throwing the leaders into solitary confinement, and firing the hunger strikers from their jobs at the detention center, which they relied on to pay for phone calls, sanitary pads, and other necessities.[91] The Department of Justice under the Obama administration asserted that much like John Turner, these immigrants had no First Amendment rights because they had never been admitted to the United States.[92]

The historical context surrounding the Immigration Act of 1903 and the Turner case demonstrates a pattern in US political history: a tragedy, like the murder of President McKinley, is wrongfully attributed to people of color or immigrants; and the response to that tragedy puts a bull's-eye on the wrong culprit, triggering the passage of laws and actions that scapegoat immigrants and that have deeply harmful consequences. Perhaps the most significant example of this pattern is the 9/11 terror attack, perpetrated by lawfully present foreigners on American soil, which the US government utilized to round up, detain, and deport fourteen thousand Muslim immigrants who had no ties to the attackers nor to any other terror group.[93] As a presidential candidate, Trump was quick to blame "radical Islamic terrorism" for one of the deadliest mass shootings in American history, at an LGBT nightclub in Orlando, Florida.[94] Even as president, Trump continues to invoke terrorism in order to advance his plans to build a wall along the southern border of the United States, despite a total lack of evidence that terrorists are trying to gain entry into the United States disguised as asylum seekers.[95]

John Turner's case also set the stage for the 1919 Palmer Raids, during which the US government hunted down, interrogated, detained, and deported many Jewish immigrants and union organizers under the guise of anarchism.[96] And the case also formed the basis to exclude and deport alleged socialists, communists, anarchists, leftist labor organizers, and war resisters from the United States for decades to come.

Emma Goldman

Towards the end of World War I, a great period of labor unrest began in the United States. Following the Bolshevik revolution in Russia, American politicians started to fear that a foreign revolution might find support and spread to the United States through new immigrants from Eastern Europe, and they particularly began to target Jews, many of whom were working class immigrants. One such immigrant was Emma Goldman, whose notoriety was unparalleled by any other woman at the time, and even to this day.

Born in 1869 in Kovno, Russia (present day Kaunas, Lithuania), Emma Goldman immigrated to the United States in 1885 at the age of sixteen.[97] As a child, her family had been displaced from Kovno to Germany by anti-Semitic violence. Her own migration from Germany to the United States was in response to her father's belief that Goldman did not need further education as a girl. Together, her experience of anti-Semitic violence and the restrictions placed on her as a woman informed her lifelong advocacy.

An influential feminist and well-known anarchist of her day, Emma Goldman was an early advocate of free speech, reproductive rights, women's liberation, and workers' rights. The United States alleged that her speeches led to the assassination of President McKinley, and wanted to deport her, but Goldman had been naturalized through her marriage to a US citizen, and hence the Bureau of Immigration could not deploy the Turner precedent against her for being an anarchist, because US citizens could not be deported for their ideology.

Goldman frequently gave incendiary speeches in support of anarchism and she was often arrested and indicted for them.[98]

"It is ridiculous to think that society cannot get along without government. We will say to the government: 'Give us what belongs to us in peace, and if you don't give it to us in peace, we will take it by force.' As long as I live, and am able to explain myself, I will be opposed to government, and as I live and as my brain dictates, will use force against the government."

—Emma Goldman, excerpt from her
speech in 1907[99]

Unlike Turner, Goldman was no pacifist (and even tried to assassinate a man in her early years) but she had a profound impact on many progressives and radical thinkers of her time. Roger Baldwin, who heard Goldman speak on anarchy, went on to create the American Civil Liberties Union (ACLU). Goldman also struck up a friendship with Margaret Sanger, widely regarded as the mother of reproductive rights, who established organizations that evolved into Planned Parenthood.

When the United States entered World War I, Goldman organized against the forced military conscription of young men, arguing in her anarchist publication, *Mother Earth*, that the war was a capitalist venture launched at the expense of workers' rights. Along with her long-time associate Alexander Berkman, Goldman was arrested and charged for producing anti-conscription literature.[100] Goldman and Berkman were imprisoned for two years, with the possibility of eventual deportation.[101]

> "So no great idea in its beginning can ever be
> within the law. How can it be within the law?
> The law is stationary. The law is fixed. The law
> is a chariot wheel which binds us all regardless
> of conditions or circumstances or place or time.
> The law does not even make an attempt to go into
> the complexity of the human soul which drives a
> man to despair or to insanity, out of hunger, or out
> of indignation, into a political act. But progress
> is ever changing, progress is ever renewing,
> progress has nothing to do with fixity. And in its
> place and in its time every great ideal for human
> reconstruction, for a reconstruction of society
> and the regeneration of the race—every great
> idea was considered extralegal, illegal, in its time
> and place."

—Emma Goldman during her criminal trial in 1917

While she was imprisoned, the United States enacted the Anarchist Exclusion Act of 1918, which authorized the expulsion of noncitizens who believed in or advocated the overthrow by force or violence of the Government of the United States or of all forms of law.[102] After her release from prison in

1919 at the height of the Red Scare, a young J. Edgar Hoover working at the Justice Department sought to deny Goldman's claim to US citizenship as a means to deport her.[103]

When she was young, Goldman had met and married Jacob Kershner, a young Jewish immigrant and factory worker, and had acquired her US citizenship through him. Kershner himself had obtained citizenship by showing that he had lived in the US for at least five years. In 1908, without holding any hearings or allowing Kershner to defend himself, the Bureau of Immigration revoked Kershner's citizenship, alleging that he had lied about his length of residence in the United States prior to naturalizing.[104] The Bureau of Immigration further held that because Kershner was never a US citizen, therefore Goldman could not have obtained her citizenship through marriage to him, even though she, too, never received a hearing. Faced with deportation, Goldman waived her right to an appeal.[105] Along with many others of Russian descent, she was deported in 1919.

Deportation did not lessen her notoriety. Goldman lived in Russia for a couple years before moving to Sweden, then Germany, France, and finally to England, where she met and married James Colton, a Scotch coal miner, and gained British citizenship.[106] She spoke out against Lenin, Stalin, Hitler, and all forms of totalitarianism. In 1934, fifteen years after she had been deported, she was given permission to reenter the United States to lecture on "The German Regime."[107] When asked if deportation had changed her mind, Goldman quipped, "No, I was always considered bad; I'm worse now."[108]

For her entire life until her death in 1940, Goldman participated in the social and political movements of her age, from the Russian Revolution to the Spanish Civil War.

Goldman stood out as a Jewish Russian radical, and in the eyes of many people, she was never able to overcome her foreignness. Along with the experiences of many other immigrant radicals of her time, her deportation demonstrates the federal government's intent and determination to use immigration laws to target and exclude radical immigrants, even if they are American citizens.

While less than 1,250 people were deported between 1911 and 1940 because of their political beliefs,[109] the raw numbers do not reveal the chilling effect that the Palmer Raids and later crackdowns had on dissent on by noncitizens.

Marcus Garvey

> **"[The assassination of Malcolm X] was the
> most significant loss in the history of the Black
> Movement since Marcus Garvey was deported
> back in the 1920s."**

—From the epilogue of *The Autobiography
of Malcolm X*

During World War I, the United States enlisted over four
million men into active duty. The loss of such labor from the
domestic market created a huge shortage of workers, and the
country found itself calling upon both immigrants and African
Americans to fill the labor shortage. In what became known
as The Great Migration, nearly one million African Americans
migrated north in search of a better life, escaping Jim Crow
laws in the South while making themselves an integral part of
the northern economies.[110]

White workers balked at the increase in economic competition.
White supremacists saw this as a window of opportunity,
and grew from a handful to six million members by 1925,
carrying out mass lynching and terror campaigns against black
communities across the country.[111]

Black leaders were at odds over how to achieve liberation from the violence of Jim Crow and segregation. Three different schools of thoughts emerged from this crisis—legal reformers, black socialists, and those focused on communal self-help for the black diaspora (black nationalists).[112]

Founded in 1910, the National Association for the Advancement of Colored People (NAACP) was the preeminent organization representing lobbyist reformers, who believed that equal rights could be advanced through legal reforms and by pressuring the government to ensure civil rights for all African Americans. During this era, the organization had only one black executive, W.E.B. Dubois, and its white leadership viewed African American unity or empowerment as divisive.[113]

After the Russian revolution of 1917, several African American leaders began to embrace socialism as a way to change the dynamics of racial and economic oppression in the United States. Led by A. Phillip Randolph and Chandler Owen, black socialists generally believed that solidarity among the working class was the best way of advancing economic and racial justice for African Americans.[114]

Marcus Garvey subscribed to the communal self-help model of racial liberation. Garvey grew up in Jamaica and, in his twenties, upon finding limited employment opportunities, traveled through Europe, South America, and Central America looking for work.[115] During his travels abroad, Garvey observed that people of African descent always found themselves at the bottom of every country's socioeconomic ladder. Garvey returned to Jamaica and in 1914 founded the Universal Negro Improvement Association (UNIA), which went on to become the largest membership organization of people of African descent, with nine hundred branches by 1921 in the United States alone.[116] The UNIA advocated black unity, a mass migration to Africa, and the liberation and unification of Africa as a homeland for all black people. Garvey's primary goal was to organize people of African descent across the world to become independent before seeking civil or racial integration.

Garvey came to the United States to spread his vision of black economic independence. Here, he created the Negro Factories Corporation and Black Star Line Steamship Corporation to facilitate trade and immigration for people of African descent. His vision for social entrepreneurship among black people spread like wildfire. The meteoric rise of Marcus Garvey and the Black Star Line intensified competition among African American leaders who held competing visions of black liberation. The NAACP saw their membership decreasing and blamed it on Garvey's rise to prominence.[117] Instead of debating Garvey and risk seeing his vision of black liberation become the norm, African American politicos and the white leadership of the NAACP conspired to remove him from the United States.[118]

The NAACP, A. Phillip Randolph, and Chandler Owen came together to form "Friends of Negro Freedom," with the joint goal of getting rid of Marcus Garvey.[119] Under the auspices of Friends of Negro Freedom, they created the *"Garvey Must Go!"* campaign, which provided the United States government with fodder to prosecute, convict, and deport Garvey.[120] The *Garvey Must Go!* coalition mounted a racist and xenophobic media campaign decrying Garvey as a supporter of the Ku Klux Klan, characterizing him as a leader of only "the West Indian peasantry," and accused him of undermining civil rights by trying to ship black people back to Africa.[121] These lobbyists used their power and prestige to request the United States Attorney General to arrest, indict, and convict Marcus Garvey on dubious counts of mail fraud.[122]

> **"Every man who apologizes for or defends Marcus Garvey from this day forth writes himself down as unworthy of countenance of decent Americans. As for Garvey himself, this open ally of the Ku Klux Klan should be locked up or sent home."**
>
> —W.E.B. Dubois[123]

Under dubious legal circumstances, Garvey was sentenced to five years in prison and fined a thousand dollars for fraudulent use of mail in association with the Black Star line.[124] Thousands of African Americans, including Garvey's purported victims, signed petitions and protested his conviction.[125] In response to these protests, President Coolidge commuted Garvey's sentence in 1927, and he was immediately deported.[126] The UNIA fell apart as a result of a crisis in leadership, and Garvey's dream of black liberation never came to pass.

Deportation was used to silence Garvey and his vision for black people, rather than through open debate and disagreement. Decades after his death, the popular narrative surrounding Garvey continues to be the one shepherded by those who were so threatened by the power of his vision that they worked with the US government to target, vilify, and deport him. This is not to say that Garvey was the perfect black visionary; he certainly had his faults. Part of the reason the UNIA fell apart is because Garvey refused to pass on the baton to his spouse, Amy Euphemia Jacques Garvey, a pioneering Black immigrant leader in her own right. In fact, in her book *Garvey and Garveyism*, Ms. Garvey alleges that a significant amount of Garvey's speeches were a direct result of her own work.[127] Whether this is true or not, Marcus Garvey's deportation continues to tarnish the legacy of one of the most prominent black civil rights organizations in US history.

The idea that advocacy organizations today would work in tandem with the United States government to detain and deport political dissenters is not unheard of in recent years. Indeed, during the Obama administration, former Member of Congress Luis Gutiérrez (D-IL) publicly vilified undocumented immigrant rights activist Mohammad Abdollahi, and outed him as a gay man in order to undermine public support for the "Dream 9"—a bold action to bring deported people back to the United States.[128] He was hardly alone. Along with several immigration organizations, a former American Immigration Lawyers Association (AILA) president and board member of a national immigration reform organization orchestrated a public relations blitz to undermine the legitimate asylum claims of immigrant rights activists so that they would be deported.[129] Many of these activists won their claims; but many remain in deportation proceedings.

Garvey's story is a reminder that people can be intentionally and unjustly tarnished, degraded, and banished for political purposes, and that unless we learn the truth about the past, and pledge to heed the lessons we find there, we are bound to repeat the same mistakes in the present and future.

Alfred Renton Bridges ("Harry Bridges")

"There is a weapon we can fight with. That is the weapon of political action."

—Harry Bridges

Few people know of Alfred Renton Bridges, or Harry Bridges as he liked to be called, but once upon a time, the United States government spent twenty years trying to deport him for his labor rights activism. Unlike Turner, Goldman, or Garvey, his story is one of triumph, though at great personal and political cost.

Through the Emergency Quota Act of 1921, Congress limited the number of immigrants allowed entry annually to 3 percent of the number of residents from that same country living in the United States according to the US Census of 1910.[130]Congress followed with the even more restrictive Immigration Act of 1924 (the Johnson-Reed Act), which imposed a total annual quota of 165,000, with a limit of 2 percent of each nationality as recorded in the 1890 census.[131] This meant that people from northern European countries were more likely to be admitted to the US than people from Eastern Europe or Southern Europe because most immigration from there occurred after 1890.[132]

During the 1930s Great Depression and World War II, Congress continued to ramp up efforts to deport or exclude immigrants on ideological grounds. Groups of newly arriving immigrants were targeted one day but approved of the next, only to be replaced by another allegedly dangerous immigrant group. While the treatment of US citizens accused of communism during the McCarthy era (1940s–1950s) was horrendous, the treatment of noncitizens accused of similar political sympathies was even worse.

Hailing from Australia, Alfred Renton Bridges arrived in the United States in 1920 as a nineteen-year-old through the Merchant Marines. Bridges was a staunch proponent of left-wing unions, and ultimately found work on the docks in San Francisco, California. His involvement in the 1934 West Coast Waterfront Strike, where workers shut down ports along the West Coast and successfully unionized for better working conditions is what angered his political opponents.[133]

Responding to political pressure from several sources including right-wing newspapers, the shipping industry lobby, Hoover's FBI, members of the House Un-American Activities Committee, and the American Legion, in 1938 the federal government instituted deportation proceedings against Bridges. The government alleged that he had been a member of or was affiliated with the Communist Party.[134] By then, Bridges had founded the International Longshore and Warehouse Union(ILWU), thereby expanding membership to workers in warehouses. However, the hearing examiner at the US Department of Labor, which used to have jurisdiction over immigration matters, concluded that the evidence did not support the charge.[135]The Supreme Court had held in an earlier case that former membership in the Communist Party was not a grounds for deportation,[136] and Bridges seemed to have no current membership. [137]

After failing to deport Bridges in 1939, Congress enacted the Alien Registration Act of 1940, known as the Smith Act, to allow the deportation of a noncitizen who at any time had been a member of any organization advocating violence as a way to overthrow the government or who was affiliated with any organization that advocated the same.[138] On this new basis, once again, the United States tried to deport Bridges. This time, the hearing officer held that the Marine Workers' Industrial Union was affiliated with the Communist Party, which allegedly did want to violently overthrow the government. The Board of Immigration Appeals disagreed with the hearing officer's assertion.[139] But the Attorney General overruled the Board and ordered Bridges deported.

Bridges then appealed the case to the US Supreme Court, which ruled in his favor in 1945, finding that the evidence of his communist membership was exceedingly tenuous.[140] Agreeing with the majority, Justice Frank Murphy wrote:

> **"Seldom if ever in the history of this nation has there been such a concentrated and relentless crusade to deport an individual because he dared to exercise the freedom...that is guaranteed to him by the Constitution... For more than a decade, powerful economic and social forces have combined with public and private agencies to seek the deportation of Harry Bridges."**

Bridges was naturalized as a US citizen three months later.[141] That should have put an end to the matter. However, in 1949, the US government accused him of committing fraud and perjury because Bridges had claimed at his citizenship hearing that he had never been a communist.[142] Armed with dubious witnesses, the government began criminal proceedings against Bridges and his union associates, and finally earned a criminal conviction and began the process of denaturalizing him.[143] This conviction was subsequently reversed by the US Supreme Court in 1953 on the technicality that the government had not brought the allegations of fraud against Bridges within the required three-year statute of limitations.[144]

Bridges avoided deportation and died in San Francisco in 1990 at the age of eighty-nine.[145] His trials and tribulations serve as a reminder that immigrants have always been blamed for bringing "radical ideology" into the United States and disrupting existing harmonious relationships between capital and labor. Cast as un-American for daring to challenge the status quo, radical immigrants have long been red-baited and ostracized from popular movements in order to impede social change.

Many forces still try to pit US citizens and noncitizen immigrants against each other, but the life and trials of Harry Bridges illustrate the potential for social change when workers stop fighting over crumbs and unite.

Luisa Moreno and the Santa Ana Four

The long-standing effort to deport Harry Bridges did not succeed, but during the Cold War, the United States continued to brand and target community organizers as subversive communists in order to quash and deport dissent. The number of noncitizens apprehended or excluded from the United States quadrupled between 1946 and the early 1950s.[146] Even citizens of the United States faced immigration enforcement.

At the beginning of the Cold War, the United States passed the Internal Security Act of 1950, which required communist organizations to register with the Attorney General and established the Subversive Activities Control Board to investigate people suspected of communist affiliations.[147] Noncitizens belonging to subversive groups could not become US citizens, and in some cases, were threatened with deportation. US Citizens who switch around to had previously participated in groups deemed subversive could have their citizenship revoked, could not get federal jobs, and were rendered ineligible for passports.[148]

Contrary to popular opinion, noncitizens targeted for subversive activities during the Cold War were not just Eastern European. Indeed, long before the legend of Cesar Chavez and

Dolores Huerta, Latino labor leaders, such as Luisa Moreno, Josefina Fierro, and Bert Corona, proudly embraced left-wing, multi-racial labor organizing while fighting against the deportation terror and the vestiges of white supremacy.

The history of xenophobia against Latinx Americans, and the organizing in response to it predates the Cold War. During the Great Depression, the United States arrested, detained, and deported many Mexicans and Mexican Americans to make space in the workforce for those perceived as white American.[149] In response to Immigration and Nationalization Service (INS) raids and deportations, Mexican American workers joined forces with other labor organizers, including many communist-affiliated organizations. Over the course of a couple decades, it became increasingly difficult to separate the issue of Latinx labor organizing from communism.

Luisa Moreno, a Guatemalan immigrant, stands out as one of the more notable and respected labor organizers during this era. She organized garment workers in New York, cigar workers in Florida, cannery workers in California, and with Josefina Fierro and Bert Corona founded the Spanish-Speaking Congress in order to address the needs of laborers with limited English proficiency.[150] By the time INS officials came to seek her deportation in 1949 as a "dangerous alien," she had already retired from union and political work.[151]

INS contended that Moreno was dangerous because she had belonged to a communist organization during the 1930s that allegedly advocated the overthrow of the government by force or violence, and they detained Moreno at Terminal Island while she awaited deportation.[152] Unfortunately, the committee that organized to help defend her failed to prevent her voluntary departure to Guatemala, but it did inspire the creation of the Los Angeles Committee for the Protection of the Foreign Born (LACPFB).

The LACPFB was a partner organization of the larger New York based American Committee for the Protection of the Foreign Born (ACPFB), which was considered subversive by the United States government because it protected foreign-born radicals, communists, and labor organizers. Both organizations made no distinction between workers with or without proper documents, and condemned the raids and deportations as fascism and police-state terror.[153] The organizations raised money for bail, provided legal support to those caught up in the deportation quagmire, mobilized mass support against deportations, and provided the families of deportees with basic necessities.[154]

With the passage of the Immigration and Nationality Act of 1952 (McCarran-Walter Act), Congress broadened the category of people it could target for deportation to include noncitizens who spoke or wrote in support of radical ideologies at any time in their lives.[155] Massive INS raids followed in the 1950s, many directed toward immigrants who had organized with labor unions in the past. The case of the "Santa Ana Four" (Justo Cruz, Andreas González, Agustín Esparza, Elias Espinoza) best represents the targeting of Mexican American workers for their political associations, and how the LACPFB helped to fight back.

Justo Cruz and Elias Espinoza got on the radar of US immigration officials as former members of the Worker's Alliance, which had fought for jobs and better working conditions during the Great Depression of the 1930s.[156] The organization no longer existed, but Cruz continued to be active in the community as a member of the Orange County Community Chest, a collective of civic groups that had played a crucial role in desegregating schools for Mexican American children.[157]

> **"If a man is 'dangerous' because he thinks that wages should allow the worker and his family to have enough to eat and live in a decent home, then I'll agree—Justo Cruz is a very 'dangerous' man."**
>
> —Ladislo Cruz, son of Justo Cruz on his father's arrest and detention

US immigration officials threatened Cruz's livelihood first by complaining about him to his employer. Failing to get him fired, INS arrested him on October 17, 1951, along with Elias Espinoza, Agustín Esparza, and Andreas González, and charged them all under the Internal Security Act for failing to register as communists.

There is little doubt that the four men had been affiliated with communism in the 1930s. But by the time INS detained the Santa Ana Four, they had lived in Orange County for several decades, had US citizen spouses and children, and had built their entire lives in the United States.

Cruz and the others were sent to San Pedro's Terminal Island, where other immigrants suspected of subversive activities awaited deportation. Bail was set at an excessive amount, but when their families found out about their arrest and detention, they banded together with the LACPFB to raise over sixteen thousand dollars to bail them out.[158]

The LACPFB and the families of the Santa Ana Four worked together to collect thousands of signatures to stop their impending deportation. Lawyers for the LACPFB worked tirelessly to defend them. Besides providing legal support, the LACPFB also published educational pamphlets about the Santa Ana Four to generate support and combat government propaganda.[159] Alas, Gonzales and Esparza turned themselves in for deportation in 1953.[160] Espinoza was also ordered deported in 1964.[161] Only Cruz won a stay of deportation because he was the sole provider of his two US citizen children.[162]

Anti-Mexican and anti-radical hysteria permeated the 1950s and created a chilling effect on people's willingness to associate with left-wing organizations. The United States government targeted members of the LACPFB and similar coalitions, not just to combat communism but also to dissuade more workers from joining these organizations and exercising their right to freedom of speech and expression. Over time, the crucial work of the LACPFB was forgotten, and never made it into the history books. As the United States faces a new era of ideology-based deportations and exclusions of noncitizens, we need to emulate the bravery of the LACPFB and fight back as they once did.

Rose Chernin

> **"The things we take for granted now, part of the American way of life, these were revolutionary ideas when we began to demand them in the thirties. We wanted unemployment insurance; we wanted home relief, hot meals for children in schools, and housing for the destitute people living in the city dumps."**

—Rose Chernin in "Organizing the Unemployed in the Bronx in the 1930s" (1949)

The LACPFB emerged from the multi-racial communities of Los Angeles, most notably from Boyle Heights. Rose Chernin, a Jewish immigrant, helped to create and became the executive director of the LACPFB in 1950.

Rose Chernin was born in Russia in 1901 as Rochelle Chernin.[163] She was driven into political advocacy through a series of displacements. Her father left her mother when she was a young child, and in 1913, when she was only twelve years old, she and her mother immigrated to the United States.[164] She was naturalized as a US citizen in 1929, and joined the Communist Party in 1932.[165]

During the Great Depression, Chernin was active in the anti-eviction protests in Bronx, New York, supporting rent strikes and rent control.[166] Later, she moved to Boyle Heights, Los Angeles, where she started to organize foreign-born workers of all backgrounds and created the LACPFB. Chernin and the people she recruited for the LACPFB recognized that immigrant rights were connected to racial and economic justice.[167] Therefore the LACPFB grew to be a diverse, multiracial coalition of Jewish, Latinx, and Asian immigrant organizers.

In 1951, the Immigration and Naturalization Service tried to deport Chernin because of her political ideology and work with the LACPFB. The US government began criminal proceedings against her, alleging that she was part of a conspiracy to overthrow the US government by force and violence.[168] Chernin was convicted for teaching and advocating communism, and then denaturalized so that she could be deported to the Soviet Union.[169] Using her conviction, the United States revoked Chernin's citizenship on the grounds that she had entered the country fraudulently when she was a child to become a communist agent.

Fortunately for Chernin and other members of the Communist Party who were tried with her, in 1957 the Supreme Court of the United States ruled 6–1 in favor of overturning their convictions.[170] The Court clarified that convictions under the Smith Act required proof of "forcible action" to overthrow the government rather than mere advocacy of revolutionary politics.[171] In doing that, the Court severely limited the application of the Smith Act, and this marked the end of prosecutions based on Communist Party membership.

The Smith Act trials decimated both the LACPFB and the Communist Party in the United States. While Chernin avoided deportation, many rank and file leaders were fined, arrested, convicted, and deported because of their affiliations with the Party. Those who supported the values espoused by the Communist Party feared being targeted in a similar way and distanced themselves from the Party.

Although the Supreme Court weakened the Smith Act, Congress never repealed it. The government maintains the power to exclude anyone who seeks to enter to engage in "espionage or sabotage," in "any other unlawful activity," or in "any activity [opposing the US government] by force, violence, or other unlawful means."[172] The Immigration and Nationality Act continues to prohibit naturalization for anyone who has been part of a group that advocates or teaches violence as a way of overthrowing the government or who is involved with the Communist Party or any other totalitarian party.[173]

As we will see later, when the United States could no longer deport people based on political ideology or membership in the Communist Party, they switched to claiming that people were threats to national security.

Ellen Knauff

By the 1950s, it was established that under the pretext of national security the government had the power to deport anyone. Besides using this power against political advocates, the United States also wielded it against virtually anyone for any reason.

Ellen Knauff was born in Germany in 1915.[174] During the reign of Hitler, Knauff's parents and other Jewish relatives perished in the Nazi camps. Knauff fled to to Czechoslovakia (now Czech Republic), where she married and later divorced. After the war, she came back to Germany and worked as a civilian employee for the United States Army. In 1948 she married a United States citizen and Army veteran, Kurt Knauff, whom she had met while he was stationed abroad. She came to the United States to apply for naturalization under a new law, the War Brides Act.[175] But upon her entry, she surprisingly was detained at Ellis Island. She was denied admission according to a presidential proclamation that allowed a noncitizen to be excluded if his or her entry "would be prejudicial to the interests of the United States" during wartime.[176]

At Ellis Island, Knauff was never afforded a hearing and never told the reason for her exclusion, though officials did hint later that they considered her a spy because of the time she had spent in Czechoslovakia and her prior marriage to a Czech.[177]

She was detained on the island for over three years awaiting a decision.[178] After the Supreme Court predictably decided in favor of the government, a public outcry ensued.

Newspapers condemned the Court's ruling. The St. Louis Post-Dispatch and the New York Post mounted publicity campaigns for Knauff, prompting several members of Congress to introduce private bills on her behalf, even as the Attorney General of the United States rushed to deport her.[179] A stay of deportation from Justice Jackson came only moments before she was scheduled to board her flight.[180]

Public pressure and support through private bills allowed Knauff to reopen her case while remaining in the United States.[181] She was finally afforded a full hearing. The government alleged that they sought to exclude her on security grounds because Knauff had engaged in espionage while working for the US Army in Germany.[182] The main evidence against Ms. Knauff came from a previously scorned lover of her current husband, who claimed that Knauff was a communist.[183] She lost the initial hearing, and was once again detained at Ellis Island until the board agreed with her appeal, and granted her permanent residence. Her difficulties were not over, however. Two years later, when Knauff applied for citizenship in the United States, her interviewing officer accused her of being a communist spy.[184]

Knauff's case cemented the exclusive authority of the US government to refuse admission of anyone into the United States, no matter how dubious the reason. However, the case also underscores the potential power of the public in changing the outcome of a case. After the Supreme Court decided her case, Congress sought to assist Ellen Knauff, and the press upbraided the government's actions.

Over time, the Supreme Court has upheld the power of the Executive Branch to exclude people for any bona fide reason. For example, in *Kleindienst v. Mandel*, the Supreme Court refused to overrule the Attorney General's decision to exclude a Belgian editor of a socialist publication from entering the United States to lecture at an academic conference.[185]

To this day, the Executive Branch can revoke refugee status, deny entry or a visa without regard to due process of law. Days after Donald Trump took office in 2017, he signed an executive order that suspended the US refugee resettlement program for 120 days and that banned the entry of lawful permanent residents, refugees, visitors, and students from some Muslim-majority countries (Iran, Iraq, Yemen, Syria, Sudan, Libya, and Somalia).[186]

Due to a public outcry from people who rushed to airports across the country, and because of the ensuing litigation, significant portions of this ban and later versions were blocked by federal courts, who found each iteration to be blatantly anti-Muslim, unconstitutional, and an abuse of the president's power. But on June 26, 2018, the US Supreme Court upheld the legality of a revised version of the travel ban in *Trump v. Hawaii*, citing the *Mandel* decision, and concluding that the president was lawfully exercising the broad authority granted to him to suspend the entry of certain noncitizens into the United States.[187]

While she was eventually triumphant, Knauff's story serves as a reminder as to why we should not take at face value claims by the executive branch about secret evidence and national security threats.

John Lennon

The government has not spared even famous celebrities from ideological-based exclusions or deportations. A legendary member of the Beatles, not many people know that John Lennon was specifically targeted for deportation after he protested the US involvement in the Vietnam War.

While not an advocate in the traditional sense, many today regard former Beatles musician, John Lennon, as an anti-war activist for the way he used his craft and celebrity status to encourage social and political change.

Knowing their wedding would garner much publicity, John Lennon and his wife, Yoko Ono, decided to use the event to promote peace and dialogue to help end the war in Vietnam. Spun off the concept of "sit-in" protest, in 1969, Lennon and Ono invited the press to their honeymoon in Amsterdam, where they sat in bed for two consecutive weeks, between nine in the morning and nine at night, having discussions about peace in the world.[188] During a second similar "protest" in Montreal, John Lennon wrote and later recorded "Give Peace a Chance," which turned into the universal chant that was used at the demonstrations against the war in Vietnam.[189]

> **"Imagine all the people living life in peace. You may say I'm a dreamer, but I'm not the only one. I hope someday you'll join us, and the world will be as one."**
>
> —John Lennon

Lennon wanted to conduct the second "bed-in" protest in New York, but he was not allowed to enter the United States because of a conviction for possession of cannabis resin that had allegedly been planted on him by a police officer.[190] However, Lennon was admitted into the United States in August 1971, along with Ono, to seek custody of Ono's daughter from a previous marriage.[191] While in the United States, Lennon planned an anti-Nixon concert tour, which caught the attention of authorities.[192]

In response to his advocacy, an increasingly paranoid Nixon White House placed Lennon under surveillance, wiretapped him through the FBI, and ordered the INS to deport Lennon and Ono from the United States.[193] The political nature of Lennon's deportation case can be gleaned from the involvement of the FBI leadership in this case. FBI Director J. Edgar Hoover expressed concern that Lennon might not be deported before the 1972 Republican National Convention. A memorandum from Acting FBI Director Gray stated that an arrest on narcotics charges would insure immediate deportation. A memorandum to Senator Strom Thurmond and Attorney General John Mitchell stated that termination of Lennon's visa would be a "strategic countermeasure" against the anti-war and anti-Nixon movement.[194]

Lennon's visa expired in 1972, and he tried to obtain lawful permanent resident status, but the INS instituted deportation proceedings against him based on the 1968 drug conviction.[195] Through his lawyers, Lennon fought deportation by asserting that the INS had a secret program of prosecutorial discretion program, called the "non-priority program," which could allow him to stay in the United States as a low-priority individual.[196] At the time, the INS denoted it as "non-priority status" and publicly denied its existence.[197] The fact that the INS did not use this program to help Lennon stay in the US was further confirmation that this was selective prosecution. Even the Second Circuit Court of Appeals noted Lennon's selective prosecution when they finally used other grounds to overturn his deportation order. After Nixon's resignation, Lennon was finally granted a lawful permanent residency under the Ford administration.

Lennon's deportation battle revealed the INS practice of using prosecutorial discretion (or "deferred action," as they later dubbed it) to allow certain noncitizens to avoid deportation. Although the INS rescinded the guidance in 1997, today Department of Homeland Security (DHS) officials continued to apply the same humanitarian factors in deciding whether to grant an individual deferred action.[198] And advocates continued to seek deferred action for their clients as a last-ditch effort to keep a noncitizen in the United States.

The United States soon began to offer categorical deferred action to certain groups, such as the abused spouses and children of lawful permanent residents and US citizens, victims of crimes in the US, foreign students impacted by Hurricane Katrina, and the widow(er)s of US citizens.[199] In June 2012, the Obama administration implemented a deferred action program for undocumented youth who came to the United States as children, called DACA.[200] In many ways, we have Lennon and his advocacy to thank for these programs. Without his battle with INS, we might never have known about the existence of the non-priority or deferred action program.

Los Angeles Eight

As the Cold War waged on, exclusions based on political ideology remained in place. Under the 1952 McCarran-Walter Immigration and Nationality Act, the US government excluded many prominent foreign nationals who sought to visit the United States, such as Pablo Neruda, Carlos Fuentes, Gabriel García Márquez, Regis Debray, Ernst Mandel, Dario Fo, and even Pierre Trudeau.[201] In 1984, the INS estimated that around eight thousand people from ninety-eight countries had been excluded from the United States based on their political beliefs.[202]

After Congress restricted the powers granted to the Executive Branch to deport people based on their political beliefs, the government started to deploy the terrorist rubric to continue ideology-based exclusions and deportations. Perhaps nothing exemplifies the changing bogeyman in American politics better than the case of the Los Angeles Eight.

Under the Reagan Administration, the INS created the "Alien Terrorists and Undesirables: A Contingency Plan," which suggested using the McCarran-Walter Act to apprehend and detain noncitizens from predominantly Arab countries and Iran.[203] In January 1987, INS agents arrested and detained eight people—seven Palestinian activists and one Kenyan— under the McCarran-Walter Act, charging them for reading and redistributing pro-Palestinian literature that was linked to the Popular Front for the Liberation of Palestine ("PFLP"). All of them denied membership or affiliation with the PFLP. All were detained for twenty-three days in a maximum-security prison in solitary confinement for supporting a terrorist organization.[204] This began an epic twenty-year battle to try and prove that the eight men were terrorists and should be deported.

The LA 8—Amjad Obeid, Ayman Obeid, Khader Hamide, Julie Mungai Hamide, Bashar Amer, Nairn Sharif, Michel Shehadeh, and Iyad Barakat—were all lawfully present in the United States, living normal lives as students, parents, and spouses.[205] They were also part of broader progressive movements and moved quickly to organize support for themselves.[206] As the case progressed and the government submitted thousands of pages as evidence, it became clearly evident that the LA 8 were being targeted for their progressive viewpoints.[207] In the first of many victories for the LA 8, a federal district court judge rejected the government's contentions and struck down the ideological exclusions of the McCarran-Walter Act as unconstitutional because they impinged upon constitutionally protected associational activity.[208]

Partly in response to this decision, Congress passed the Immigration Act of 1990, which narrowed the ideological exclusion grounds. As amended, the law states that a noncitizen "shall not be excludable...because of the alien's past, current, or expected beliefs, statements, or associations, if such beliefs, statements, or associations would be lawful within the United States."[209] However, Congress replaced one alleged foreign-born threat with another—it rendered deportable any noncitizen "who has engaged, is engaged, or at any time after entry engages in terrorist activity..."[210] Terrorist activity was broadly defined as providing any kind of material support to individuals or organizations.[211] For example, a noncitizen could be deported for simply raising money for a hospital, clinic, or day care center run by groups like the Salvadoran Farabundo Martí National Liberation Front (FMLN) or the African National Congress, even without any actual knowledge of or affiliation with these organizations.

Thereafter, the INS started new deportation proceedings against the LA 8 based on the new terrorism grounds, arguing that the PFLP was a terrorist organization and the LA 8 were members of the PFLP.[212] The LA 8 filed a countersuit with the help of the American-Arab Anti-Discrimination Committee (ADC), alleging that the LA 8 had been singled out for selective prosecution.[213] After a series of victories, the LA 8 were devastated when the Supreme Court agreed with the government, stating that people who were unlawfully present could not protect themselves from deportation by claiming that the government was trying to deport them for controversial viewpoints.[214] In doing so, the Supreme Court sent the case back down to the immigration court to renew deportation proceedings against the LA 8. Fortunately, a Los Angeles immigration judge finally terminated proceedings against the LA 8 in 2007 because the government had refused to present evidence that exonerated the victims.[215]

Though extreme, the government's efforts to deport the Los Angeles Eight based on their political association should not be viewed as an isolated incident. Indeed, it laid the groundwork for the government's Muslim registration program (NSEERS), and the present Muslim ban. The United States would continue to use political association as a reason to target noncitizens when a new "threat" emerged on the home front: undocumented youth activists.

Tam Tran

"I am culturally an American, and, more specifically, I consider myself a Southern Californian," Tran told a congressional House subcommittee during her testimony for the Development, Relief, and Education for Alien Minors (DREAM) Act on May 18, 2007.[216] "I grew up watching *Speed Racer* and *Mighty Mouse* every Saturday morning."[217] When Tam spoke before powerful members of the United States Congress, she made it clear that she was taking this risk to "give voice to thousands of undocumented students who could not" at the time afford to do so without fear of repercussion.[218]

Unfortunately, speaking out did not come without repercussions. Three days after this powerful testimony, and in apparent retaliation and at the urging of former Congressperson Tom Tancredo (R-CO), ICE agents staged a predawn raid on Tam's family home in Orange County and took her parents and brother into custody.[219]

Tam Tran was born to Vietnamese parents in Germany on October 30, 1982.[220] After the fall of Saigon in 1975, her family was forced to flee Vietnam by boat, along with hundreds of thousands of other refugees. While many Vietnamese refugees were rescued at sea by Americans and relocated to the United States, Tran's parents were rescued by the German navy.[221] They came to live in Germany, where Tam Tran was born. However, Germany does not confer birthright citizenship.

The Tran family came to the United States when Tam was six years old to join other family members who had settled in California.[222] Her parents applied for political asylum, but their request was denied because they had emigrated from Germany, not directly from Vietnam.

A graduate of UCLA, Tam was a gifted filmmaker who produced acclaimed documentaries, such as *Lost and Found* and *Seattle Underground Railroad*, which capture the lives of undocumented youth living surviving under brutal immigration laws. Tam used her statelessness to talk openly about the DREAM Act and speak out at various academic conferences about the need for reforms. Because of the political connections she built, she was able to seek release of her family from immigration custody when they were targeted because of her outspoken advocacy.[223]

Tam Tran was doing a PhD in American Civilization at Brown University, when she was tragically killed in a car crash in 2010, along with her friend and fellow advocate, Cynthia Felix. She was only twenty-seven years old.[224] She had hoped that the country, where she had resided for more than twenty years as a law-abiding, tax-paying student, would finally, through the passage of the DREAM Act, consider her to be an American.

Her dreams never came to pass while she was alive, but a day after her tragic death, four undocumented youth sat down in Senator John McCain's office in Arizona to ask him to cosponsor the DREAM Act.[225] Today, her courageous spirit lives on through the lives of her family members and friends, who in her stead continue to resist the deportation regime.[226]

The consequences of organizing and protesting are not the same for people who are noncitizens. Throughout history, immigrant leaders have taken many risks and shown immense political courage by coming out of the shadows and organizing to protect themselves and their communities.

As the Trump administration starts collecting data on our social media profiles,[227] this is not the time to tell immigrants to go back into the shadows or curb their advocacy, but the time to join forces and show the Trump administration that the risks that previous immigrants took were not in vain. That's what Emma Goldman, Marcus Garvey, Tam Tran, and the other change makers targeted by pretextual deportations would have wanted from us.

THE IMMIGRANT HISTORY OF SEXUALITY

●●●●●●●●●●●

Up until the latter half of the 2010s, scholars, pundits, and politicians paid scant attention to lesbian, gay, bisexual, transgender (LGBT) or queer immigrants. While both immigration and LGBT rights have been hot button issues for over half a century, up until recently, LGBT immigrants have been largely ignored, as a result of tunnel vision and exclusions built into law. An estimated 900,000 LGBT immigrants live in the US, including about 267,000 who are undocumented, according to a 2013 report from the Williams Institute at UCLA Law.[228]

Throughout much of United States history, any sexuality and gender identity that fell outside the norm of straight and cisgender has been viewed as deviant behavior and treated with ridicule, ostracism, erasure, and even genocide. In fact, up until 1990, being lesbian, gay, bisexual, and transgender could get a person deported or barred from entry to the United States.

The history of immigration law is a history of exclusion. In 1917 the United States officially began denying entry to noncitizens who were "mentally defective," had been convicted of "crimes of moral turpitude," or who were "persons of constitutional psychopathic inferiority."[229] The latter term referred to people who are now broadly perceived as queer and gender non-conforming.

The post-World War II climate created conditions for the expansion of queer culture based on how the war and, earlier, the Great Depression, had destabilized gender roles. More cohesive queer subcultures forged communities that shared a sense of self based on their same-sex sexual desires and, in some instances, based on demands for social understanding and civil rights. In response to growing visibility of queer persons, the government lumped together communist radicals and "homosexuals" as a threat to the American way of life. Senator McCarthy asserted that much like communists, "homosexuals" could also sneak undetected into the United States.

The history of discrimination based on sexuality runs deep. In 1953, following claims by Senator McCarthy that "homosexuals" had overtaken the Truman administration, President Eisenhower issued an executive order banning the employment of "homosexuals," and requiring that private contractors employing gay individuals search them out and terminate them.[230] In carrying out this order, government officials targeted, harassed, and fired hundreds of perceived queer and gender non-conforming civil servants from their government jobs, in what is now dubbed the Lavender Scare.[231] The Veterans Administration denied Government Issue (GI) benefits to service members who had been discharged because of their sexuality.[232] The policy of discriminating against LGBT individuals in federal hiring continued until the late 1990s.

Given how the state linked homosexuality and communism with foreign subversion and destabilization, it was no wonder that the United States started to exert authority over perceived sexual deviants and gender non-conforming people by turning to immigration law as a way to regulate these bodies.

Congress revised the 1952 Immigration and Nationality Act to exclude persons "afflicted with psychopathic personality" before revising it in 1965 to add "sexual deviation."[233] The law required suspected LGBT noncitizens to be sent to a public health official for examination, who would determine whether the person was indeed queer. This was a direct attack on those who were deemed transgressive and undesirable because of their gender and sexuality.

Official statistics are skewed, preventing an accurate count of the gender and sexual minorities who were deported or barred entry into the United States. Two hundred and ninety-two people were barred as "persons of constitutional psychopathic inferiority" from 1917 to 1924; 322 more were barred under this category from 1937 to 1952; and 47 were barred as having "psychopathic personality" from 1953 to 1956.[234] Many more queer people were likely deported and excluded in ways that are not evident from official statistics, such as under the categories of "likely to become a public charge" or "crimes involving moral turpitude." For example, a person who committed sodomy could be deportable or excludable merely as someone who committed a crime involving moral turpitude, without necessitating a finding of "psychopathic personality."

Although the 1990 Immigration Act eliminated the provision used to exclude sexual and gender non-conforming minorities from the United States, and the US Supreme Court struck down federal bans on same-sex marriage in 2013, challenges remain for queer immigrants in the United States.

In this chapter, we map a previously uncharted history of queer immigration. First, we discuss the lives of some individuals who were targeted by the government in the 1950s and 1960s as "psychopathic personalities" for being queer or gender non-conforming. These stories show how the government created "homosexuality" as an identity, in order to regulate same-sex relations and bodies. Next, we'll cover the advocacy against the HIV ban during the turbulent '80s from groups such as Act UP. And finally, we'll turn to the "undocuqueers"—queer undocumented leaders who have redefined the immigrant rights movement.

Together, these stories explain that while the battle to win immigration rights started in the closet for many queer immigrants, today the immigrant rights movement is led by a rich patchwork of queers, who weave politics, prose, and protest in resistance to all borders.

George Fleuti

George Fleuti was the plaintiff in the single most renowned case in immigration textbooks. What lawyers take away from the Fleuti case is the doctrine that lawful permanent residents are not making an "entry" into the United States when returning from a brief, casual, and innocent trip abroad, and therefore they cannot be held as inadmissible due to past crimes.[235] However, even those who have a solid grasp of the Fleuti doctrine do not know the story of George Fleuti. His fight against deportation is what led Congress to specifically exclude "homosexuals" from the United States.

George Fleuti, a Swiss national, became a lawful permanent resident on October 9, 1952.[236] He worked as the front office manager at the Ojai Valley Inn and Country Club. As a permanent resident, Fleuti made a brief trip to Ensenada, Mexico in August 1956, and then returned to the United States, only to be targeted for deportation. Fleuti had been convicted three years earlier in 1953 as "willfully and lawfully a dissolute person," and in 1956 for an act of oral copulation.[237] The INS tried to deport him for another arrest in 1958 (later dismissed) using the "crimes involving moral turpitude" provision, however, his deportation was set aside on the grounds that the crime he had committed was a petty offense that would not otherwise lead to deportation.

Failing to deport Fleuti in the first instance, in 1959, the INS recharged him as a noncitizen who was "afflicted with psychopathic personality," based on the fact that he had engaged in same-sex relations over a long period of time, even before he immigrated to the United States.

Fleuti challenged his deportation in district court, and when the district court upheld the decision, he appealed it to the Ninth Circuit Court of Appeals. He was represented by Hiram W. Kwan and Betty Tom Chu, pioneering Asian Americans in the legal profession. The government did not stand a chance. The Ninth Circuit found that George Fleuti had no way of knowing that practicing "homosexuality" after his initial admission to the United States could get him deported under the psychopathic personality bar. The court pointed out that a government surgeon and Fleuti's own psychiatrist disagreed as to the meaning of the term psychopathic personality. In effect, the court said that the term "psychopathic personality" was overly broad, and therefore void because it was so vague. So the court set aside his deportation.

The INS appealed to the United States Supreme Court, asserting that "homosexuality" was a condition, not just a behavior, and hence Fleuti should have been barred from entry to the United States. But while vacating the ruling of the lower court, the Supreme Court dodged the question of whether "psychopathic personality" was a broad and vague term. Perhaps their discomfort in addressing sexuality had a silver lining. Instead of answering the question of whether "psychopathic personality" was unconstitutionally vague, the Supreme Court contended that as a lawful permanent resident, Fleuti had never made a real departure by just going abroad for a brief period of time, and therefore, the INS could not charge him as excludable (because he was never seeking entry in 1956 when he returned from a brief trip abroad). Therefore, Fleuti could not be deported for either his criminal history or his sexual orientation. This piece of legal fiction continues to be good law because it means that millions of lawful permanent residents do not relinquish their right to return each time they travel abroad.

In 1965, an exasperated Congress amended the Immigration and Nationality Act to include the words "sexual deviate" to "serve the purpose of resolving any doubt on this point."[238] After two attempts to deport Fleuti, the INS then tried to deport him on grounds that he was a *constitutional psychopathic inferior* under the 1917 Act at the time of his first entry. Again, Fleuti appealed this, and in a fascinating opinion, the Board of Immigration Appeals held that he was not a "homosexual":

> **"While the records reveal that respondent has an inclination toward homosexuality, it appears to be one respondent can control and that he had it under control before he entered. Therefore, we cannot find that the record establishes that he was a homosexual at the time of that entry."**

This decision destabilized the idea of "homosexuality" as an identity by differentiating same-sex relationships from sexual identity. This was also the last attempt the government made to deport Fleuti. In 1975 Fleuti became a naturalized citizen after maintaining "more than five years of good moral character."[239]

However, while Fleuti was ultimately successful in his fight against deportation, the US government sadly succeeded in deporting many other LGBT people from the United States.

Sara Harb Quiroz

The case of Sara Harb Quiroz offers us a valuable window into the ways that border monitoring enabled the targeting of "homosexuals" by government officials with the goal of excluding LGBTQ people from the United States. While returning from a short trip to Mexico in 1960, border agents stopped Sara Harb Quiroz, a lawful permanent resident of the United States, and sent her to secondary inspection. While official records no longer exist to establish why she was stopped, her lawyer Albert Armendariz stated that it was due to the way she looked, talked, dressed, and acted.[240] Presumably, Quiroz was stereotyped as a lesbian by the border agent. She was sent to secondary inspection where she was made to sign a statement that she was a homosexual under the pretense that everything would be alright if she signed the statement.[241]

As part of the process, the INS referred her to an officer of the Public Health Service (PHS) for a medical examination. The PHS physician determined that she had a mental or physical defect as a consequence of her past same-sex behavior and issued a "Class A certificate" to the INS for Quiroz.[242] The certificate and her own statement were the evidence for exclusion at the exclusion hearing.[243]

At a subsequent removal hearing, Quiroz tried to refute her statement because she did not speak or write English and did not know what she had signed. Besides the statement (that she now challenged) where she admitted to having female lovers in the past, the INS provided testimony from Quiroz's employer who stated that Quiroz "usually wore trousers and a shirt when she came to work, and that her hair was cut shorter than some women's."[244] Quiroz argued, and several psychiatrists agreed, that even if she was a homosexual, it did not make her a psychopathic personality. She also contended that she had a nine-year-old daughter, which meant that she was not a "homosexual."

Quiroz lost the hearing. The government did not allow her to impeach her own statement. The Board of Immigration Appeals also used the fact that Quiroz had borne a child after a heterosexual relationship to advance the homophobic proposition that unfortunate experiences with a man are the reason for women to spurn further relations with other men.

When Quiroz appealed the case to the federal district court, her lawyer no longer tried to refute the finding that she was a lesbian.[245] Instead Quiroz focused on the fact that a "homosexual" was not necessarily a "psychopathic personality." The district court merely affirmed the Board of Immigration Appeals. On June 23, 1961, the Fifth Circuit Court also ruled against her and ordered her deportation by August 15, 1961.[246] However, a couple weeks before her deportation, Quiroz married Edward Escudero, and filed to reopen her case on the basis that her heterosexual marriage meant that she could not possibly be a lesbian.

However, even marriage to a man did not stop her deportation. The INS noted that even if Quiroz was now *cured* of her "homosexuality," she was deportable at the time of her entry to the United States as a "homosexual," and her marriage to a man did not change that. She was deported to Mexico in 1961.

Quiroz may not have been queer after all. Yet, her appearance as a masculine-looking woman and the government's insistence that homosexuality was an identity, not a behavior, tells us how the United States was committed to regulating any bodies that deviated from gender roles and norms. And it set the stage for the first gay deportation case to reach the Supreme Court just two years later.

Clive Boutilier

Clive Michael Boutilier, a Canadian citizen, was first admitted to the United States as a lawful permanent resident in 1955 when he was twenty-one years old.[247] In 1963, he applied for citizenship, disclosing a single arrest for a sodomy charge that had been dismissed. In 1964, after an INS interview, the Public Health Service certified that Boutilier was a "psychopathic personality, sexual deviate" at the time of his initial entry to the United States.[248] On this basis, the INS began deportation proceedings. Boutilier appealed with the help of lawyers associated with American Committee for the Protection of the Foreign Born (ACPFB), the American Civil Liberties Union (ACLU), the New York Civil Liberties Union (NYCLU), and the Homosexual Law Reform Society (HLRS). He also had the support of various psychiatrists and scientists who attested that homosexuality was not psychopathic.

Boutilier's advocates engaged in respectability politics and constructed him as a good, desirable immigrant—a hardworking farm boy who supported his family as the oldest son, who was traumatized by his parent's divorce, and victimized by his first sexual partner.[249] With respect to his sex life, his advocates noted that he had sex with both men and women, did not solicit sex, and he merely had an arrest, as opposed to a conviction.[250]

It was all to no avail. Boutilier's case was first heard by the Board of Immigration Appeals, which affirmed the INS decision in 1965, and then by the Second Circuit Court of Appeals in 1966. In 1967, the Supreme Court also ruled against Boutilier, because the Immigration and Nationality Act stated that those with a "psychopathic personality" were subject to deportation, and that the law was not void for vagueness.[251]

In 1967, Boutilier was hit by a car while crossing a street in New York, and fell into a coma for thirty days, after which he was left with brain damage.[252] He was deported to Canada on November 10, 1968, and after living in group homes for people with disabilities, he died on April 12, 2003.[253]

As a legal precedent, is largely ignored by most LGBT and immigration historians, perhaps because it has been perceived as marginal to the struggles for both LGBT and immigrant rights. This is unfortunate, because the courts started to use Boutilier to make sweeping statements about the power of Congress to exclude virtually anyone from the United States. Soon after Boutilier was deported to Canada, the sexual revolution got underway. On June 27, 1969, queer and transgender individuals in New York City responded to yet another police raid on a gay bar with several nights of rioting. The Stonewall riot (named after the bar the police raided) changed what had been an homophile accommodationist movement into an aggressive and highly effective LGBT power movement that helped revolutionize laws about sexuality.

Richard Adams and Anthony Sullivan

While immigration issues remained on the back burner for the LGBT community even after the Stonewall riots, new advocates and groups started to challenge the immigration ban from the standpoint of civil rights. Advocates from groups such as the Gay Liberation Front (GLF) demanded the American Psychiatric Association (APA) stop promoting electric shock therapy and take homosexuality out of the Diagnostic and Statistical Manual of Mental Disorders (DSM).[254] In response, the APA ruled in 1973 that "homosexuality" was not a mental disorder and removed it from the DSM.[255] The APA President John Spiegel advised the INS "to refrain from the exclusion, deportation, or refusal of citizenship to [LGBTQ migrants]," a plea that the INS ignored at the time.[256] Despite this, gay and lesbian advocates continued to challenge discriminatory laws.

Both Richard Adams and Anthony Sullivan were immigrant pioneers in the fight for marriage equality. Adams came to the United States from the Philippines when he was twelve years old and gained US citizenship in 1968 without much fanfare. It is likely that he was not profiled as a gay man and slipped under the radar of the INS.

Anthony Corbett Sullivan first entered the United States in 1971 on a multiple entry tourist visa from Australia, which is when he met Adams, who was living in Colorado.[257] Sullivan tried to maintain his visa by making short trips to Mexico, but when it finally expired in 1974, the couple obtained a marriage license in Boulder, Colorado, because a good-natured clerk was offering them to same-sex couples, and got married. Then Adams asked the INS to classify Sullivan as his spouse.

The Immigration Service denied the petition on November 24, 1975, stating that Richard Adams had "failed to establish that a bona fide marital relationship can exist between two faggots." The decision led to wide public outcry, which prompted the INS to release an equally offensive second decision:

"One of the parties to this union may function as a female in other relationships and situations but cannot function as a wife by assuming female duties and obligations inherent in the marital relationship. A union of this sort was never intended by Congress to form the basis of a visa petition."

In response to the denial of his visa petition, Adams and Sullivan sued the INS in district court, in what became the first federal lawsuit in US history seeking equal treatment for a same-sex marriage. However, besides ruling that the INS did not recognize same-sex marriage, the district court predicted that their relationship would never be recognized anywhere as a marriage.[258] Undeterred, Adams appealed to the Ninth Circuit Court of Appeals, contending that denying Sullivan an immigrant visa based on his same-sex marriage was a denial of equal protection under the law.[259] He lost again. Adams appealed to the Supreme Court, which refused to hear the case.

INS began deportation hearings against Sullivan in 1975, but his file lay dormant until the Supreme Court dismissed their final appeal. At an April 21, 1980 hearing before an immigration law judge, Sullivan requested permanent suspension of deportation because of the extreme hardship it would cause to both Adams and himself if he were deported back to Australia, where his relatives did not approve of his sexual orientation. At the time, since Sullivan had been in this country for over seven years, he was permitted to file what is known as a discretionary application for suspension of deportation. The immigration judge refused to grant him the suspension, however, and when Sullivan took it up on appeal to the Ninth Circuit, in 1985 they affirmed the decision, finalizing the deportation order.[260]

Adams and Sullivan tried at the time to seek assistance from the emerging LGBT advocacy and legal organizations, but they were shunned for fighting a losing battle and for taking things into their own hands rather than leaving the advocacy to the legal groups. At a fundraising dinner, Sullivan was confronted by a director of an LGBT organization who said to him, "Talk about a bunch of hens in a snit. We will make you understand who is in control of this movement."[261]

Despite this setback and lack of support from purported leaders, Adams and Sullivan continued to fight for marriage equality and immigration rights for four decades, never giving up hope that justice would prevail, and that the law would one day recognize them as a family. Adams and Sullivan flew to Europe where they lived for several years before coming back to the United States through the US-Mexico border. Sullivan remained in the United States as an undocumented immigrant and watched as the Defense of Marriage Act (DOMA)—which defined marriage as a union between one man and one woman—was signed into law by President Bill Clinton in September 1996. Over the years, they continued to show up at immigration protests, and increasingly so after several states started legalizing same-sex marriage in the late 2000s.

Tragically, Adams passed away in December 2012.[262] A few months later, on June 26, 2013, the US Supreme Court finally struck down a central provision of the 1996 DOMA, which had limited the federal definition of marriage to unions between one man and one woman.[263] Sullivan, now a seventy-two-year-old widower, asked the US Citizenship and Immigration Services to retroactively approve his Green Card application and automatically convert it to a widower's petition so that he could finally obtain lawful status through his late husband.[264] Much belatedly, the United States finally granted him a Green Card in 2016.[265]

Sullivan wrote to President Barack Obama, asking him to issue an apology for being called a faggot by United States Citizenship and Immigration Services (USCIS) because Adams did not deserve that rhetoric. An administration official, Leon Fresco, responded: "This agency should never treat any individual with the disrespect shown toward you and Mr. Adams. You have my sincerest apology for the years of hurt caused by the deeply offensive and hateful language used in the November 24, 1975 decision and my deepest condolences on your loss."[266]

While discriminatory policies and hurdles still exist for many binational same-sex couples, LGBT foreign nationals now may qualify for Green Cards in the United States based on their marriage to U.S. citizens and lawful permanent residents. Sullivan and Adams, pioneers in the marriage equality movement, now have one of the earliest recorded legal same-sex marriages in the modern era. Their trials helped same-sex binational couples live a little bit more freely in the United States.

Carl Hill

Around the same time that Adams and Sullivan fought for marriage equality in the 1970s and '80s, other LGBT advocates and organizations began to challenge the anti-gay exclusion ban.

When Carl Hill, a British journalist, arrived in the United States in 1979 wearing a "Gay Pride" button, immigration officials barred him from entry after Hill confirmed that he was gay.[267] With the help of Gay Rights Advocates, a San Francisco-based public interest law firm, Hill decided to take this matter to court and challenged the right of PHS officials to examine him on referral from the INS.

In response to the lawsuit, on August 2, 1979, the Surgeon General of the United States instructed PHS officers not to accept immigration referrals for medical examinations when the sole basis for the referral was to establish homosexuality as grounds for exclusion.[268] The Surgeon General concluded that "homosexuality per se will no longer be considered a mental disease or defect."[269] The following day, the Department of Justice dropped its case against Hill.[270] It began to parole suspected LGBT individuals into the United States until December 1979, when it decided that the law must be enforced, even without the availability of medical certificates.[271] The LGBT immigration ban now stood on increasingly shaky grounds that had nothing to do with science or medicine.

But the Department of Justice decided that in moving forward, it would only exclude noncitizens based on their own voluntary admission of sexual deviance or non-conforming behavior.[272] While this was an important political victory, it kept the ban in place.

Don Knutson, executive director of Gay Rights Advocates, remarked, "This case has gone past Carl Hill as an individual. [Our] purpose is to determine what authority, if any, is left to the INS to exclude [lesbians and gay men]."[273] Hill and Gay Rights Advocates contended that the 1952 McCarran-Walter Act was not enforceable because homosexuality was no longer considered a disease or mental illness, and thus, the INS could not exclude anyone as a psychopathic personality, even if they acknowledged that they were lesbian or gay.[274]

Hill's case was reopened in November of 1980, when he reentered the US and acknowledged to immigration officials that he identified as a gay man.[275] At his exclusion hearing, Hill argued that he could not be excluded without certification from PHS, and the judges agreed with him. The INS appealed, contending that the *Boutilier* precedent mandated that lesbian and gay noncitizens be excluded even without certification from PHS because their admission of homosexuality served as evidence. The BIA (Board of Immigration Appeals) sustained the appeal.[276] However, the Ninth Circuit Court of Appeals agreed that the INS required a certificate from the PHS before it could exclude a lesbian or gay man from the country.

Hill created a small crisis for the United States government. His case reverberated among a stronger, more visible LGBT community, and more visitors to the United States started to declare that they were openly gay, in order to create opposition to exclusionary rules.[277] Deportations or exclusions based on sexual orientation became more visible, and as a result, a cause for increasing protest.[278] They also posed a public relations nightmare for the United States, which at the time was the only country with such a ban. When the INS started to exclude noncitizen LGBT visitors from entering the country to attend events such as Pride, the Lesbian/Gay Freedom Day Committee, Inc. brought suit against the government.

Together with the Lesbian/Gay Freedom Day Committee, Inc., Hill once again challenged this exclusion. They contended that excluding LGBT noncitizens from entry based on their statements alone deprived them of the First Amendment right to freedom of association.[279] In a sweeping condemnation of the INS policy, the United States District Court for Northern California agreed with Hill, and issued a nationwide injunction against the LGBT exclusion, which took effect on July 26, 1982.[280]

> **"Homosexual aliens pose no threat to national security simply because they are homosexuals... The fact that some American citizens find homosexuality morally repugnant, or the purposes of the Lesbian/Gay Freedom Day events abhorrent or offensive cannot provide an important governmental interest upon which an impairment of First Amendment freedoms can be based."**

—Judge Robert Aguilar

The Ninth Circuit affirmed the decision, stating that a medical certificate was required in order to exclude gays and lesbians from the United States, and not just their own admission of sexual orientation.[281] The decision created a split between different circuit courts, as the Fifth Circuit had ruled differently on a similar issue in the case of *Longstaff*, holding that a gay man could not become a US citizen.[282] But the Supreme Court announced that it would not hear an appeal on the matter.

The Hill decision meant that future denials of entry to LGBT individuals would face serious legal scrutiny without a medical certificate, which the Surgeon General's office had already refused to provide. In response, the Senate passed an immigration reform bill that forbade lesbian and gay men turned away at the US border from challenging their exclusion in court.[283] However, the bill failed to pass the House, as advocates such as Senator Alan Cranston (CA) and Representative Barney Frank (MA)—the most prominent gay politician to date—started pressuring Congress to repeal the anti-gay immigration provision. However, it was not until the Immigration Act of 1990 that Congress finally removed the provision.[284] It was erased from law as quietly as it had been written into law.

Even after the repeal, discriminatory immigration policies that still impacted LGBT individuals were the focus of protests in 1990 during the International AIDS Conference. To further complicate matters, LGBT asylum seekers started to knock on the door, presenting a unique challenge to the American government.

LGBT Cuban Refugees

During the Cold War, relations between the United States and Cuba not only soured but almost escalated into nuclear annihilation. Cuban leader Fidel Castro (1926–2016) established the first communist state in the western hemisphere in 1959, after overthrowing the American-supported military dictatorship of Fulgencio Batista.[285] Large scale migration of Batista supporters and anti-communists from Cuba began soon after, with many choosing to flee to the United States. These Cubans were welcomed by the United States and given preferential treatment because of their symbolic value as people fleeing communism. They were often admitted or paroled into the United States for humanitarian reasons, allowed to gain lawful permanent resident status, and eventually US citizenship.

Attempts by Cubans to seek asylum in other countries escalated in April 1980 with the occupation of the Peruvian embassy in Havana, Cuba. In response, Fidel Castro announced that any Cuban wanting to leave could obtain an exit permit, though he specifically intended to direct this offer at those considered undesirable by the Cuban state. This presented a perfect opportunity for many LGBT individuals to leave Cuba, at the same time that it allowed Cuba to facilitate their exit from the country as undesirables. Some people even pretended to be gay in order to get permission to leave. Taking Castro up on the offer, roughly 125,000 people seeking freedom from his repression voyaged from Port of Mariel across the Straits of Florida to reach the United States in the remaining months of 1980.[286] This was known as the Mariel boatlift.

The sheer numbers overwhelmed the US Coast Guard. Due to Cuban propaganda, fears that many of these individuals came from mental institutions and prisons became the focus of national press coverage. In a hyperbolic gay panic, the US media reported that twenty thousand homosexuals were part of the boatlift.[287]

Conflicting immigration policies and procedures clashed, as people who were both Cuban and queer entered the United States under the glare of the media spotlight. On one hand, the United States had previously welcomed refugees from Cuba as a strategic and political ploy. On the other, the US had policies and procedures that excluded suspected homosexuals and sexual deviants. Cuban refugees who were part of the LGBT community posed a complex problem for US immigration officials who were battling challenges to gay exclusion policies. To complicate matters more, the United States did not know what to do with the hundreds of queer people who could not be returned to Cuba. The newly passed Refugee Act of 1980 did not bar entry of LGBT refugees, but the 1952 Immigration Act continued to ban "psychopathic personalities" from entering the United States.

Mariel refugees were required to have a sponsor—either a family member or a volunteer—in order to be released from US detention. It was easier to get sponsors for light-skinned refugees, young women, and those with family members in the United States than it was for queer and gender transgressive refugees. About half of the Mariel entrants were placed directly with a sponsor in South Florida.[288] The other half, the less "desirable" population, with many gender non-conforming persons, were placed in detention camps scattered across the country, as the government tried to figure out what to do with them.

Some Mariel refugees were ultimately deported, but hundreds continued to be confined in detention camps even a year later.[289] In these camps, many queer and transgender refugees were assaulted, beaten, and raped both by fellow inmates and guards.[290] Some refugees at Fort Chaffee, Arkansas and Fort Indiantown Gap, Pennsylvania demanded separate facilities due to safety issues, and circulated a petition, which stated:

"We anti-communist fighters beg of your attention to our necessity of being situated apart from the delinquents, whores, and homosexuals that are living among us. The communist government sent us together, but we are not alike."

After being ignored by the guards, many queer and transgender refugees segregated themselves voluntarily in self-defense.[291] Barrack No. 152 at Fort Chaffee in Arkansas became known as a predominantly queer and transgender camp, where detained refugees ironically found more freedom than in Cuba or the United States.[292]

The Mariel boatlift was a watershed moment in queer and transgender immigration history. Many Cuban Americans personally sailed to Cuba to pick up refugees, defying orders from the United States.[293] The Cuban refugees arrived on the heels of the 1980 Refugee Act, which created a procedure to handle and resettle refugees in the United States.[294] Under ordinary circumstances the INS still refused to admit known homosexuals, but the Carter administration granted a waiver on humanitarian grounds for lesbian and gay Cuban refugees.[295] The government worked with organizations such as the National Gay Rights Taskforce and the Metropolitan Community Church, a large queer congregation, to resettle refugees in Los Angeles and San Francisco.[296] Because the LGBT community was so welcoming, even some detained Cuban heterosexuals pretended to be gay, in order to be released from detention and resettled.[297]

Despite concerns over whether this particular group of Cuban refugees would be able to fit into the fabric of the United States, many *Marielitos* integrated successfully.[298] Notable LGBT Mariel refugees include Cuban poet and writer Reinaldo

Arenas (1943–1990), AIDS activist and television personality Pedro Zamora (1972–1994), Afro-Cuban artist Juan Boza Sánchez (1941–1991), painter Carlos Alfonzo (1950–1991), and transgender activist Adele Vázquez (1958–present). Tragically, after reaching our shores expecting freedom, many of these trailblazers died during the HIV/AIDS epidemic.

When the HIV epidemic arrived shortly after the boatlift, queer *Marielitos* (along with Haitian immigrants) were accused of spreading the epidemic.[299] With homosexuality no longer in the DSM as a mental illness, the United States turned to linking homosexuality with the AIDS epidemic, as a way of justifying the exclusion of queer and transgender immigrants from the United States, eventually imposing a total ban on immigrants with HIV.

ACT UP

"Your policies are killing me. I am dying because of you."

—ACT UP

The United States has a long and persistent history of conflating immigrants with disease as a means of excluding them. This originated with the Immigration Act of 1891, which explicitly excluded "persons suffering from a loathsome or dangerous contagious disease."[300] Officials used public health to deem people unfit for admission and citizenship. Lawmakers and public health officials created new disease categories such as "poor physique," "presenility," and "low vitality" to regulate immigrants with racial and religious differences. Even a cursory inspection of US immigration case files since 1891 reveals how public health measures like quarantine, surveillance, and behavior controls targeted people who were already disadvantaged, especially the poor, people of color, and the queer and transgender. It added a medical dimension to preexisting nativism and homophobia, utilizing fears about diseased immigrants to curb immigration from certain groups and countries.

While concern about communicable diseases is understandable, blaming Cuban or Haitian refugees and LGBT immigrants stoked fear and bigotry without saving any lives. A serious response to such a public health disaster would have left no room for fearmongering, yet the Reagan administration reacted by trying to curb refugee admissions and adding HIV as a "dangerous contagious disease" to its exclusion list.[301] This fearmongering response also directed attention away from the Reagan administration's devastatingly slow public health response to the AIDS crisis, and thousands died before Reagan even uttered the name of the disease. Until 1990, no waiver of inadmissibility was available for people living with HIV, but the stringent terms of the waiver enacted by later reforms made it almost impossible to get.[302]

The waiver required that an HIV-positive person seeking admission needed to have adequate medical treatment, private health insurance, and have a qualifying relative (spouse) who would suffer extreme hardship in the event that the person could not live in the United States. This excluded many gay noncitizens who could not prove spousal relationships because either they had not been allowed to marry or those marriages were not recognized under federal law.

Virtually all health professionals disagreed with the classification of HIV as a "communicable disease of public health significance." In fact, the United States was one of the few countries in the world with an HIV exclusion. The law initially targeted the LGBT population but also came to bar many immigrants of color, regardless of sexual orientation. Under the guise of public health, the INS started HIV testing Haitians in Florida who were applying for legalization under the Cuban-Haitian Adjustment Program, and placing them in deportation proceedings if they tested positive.[303] In the fall of 1991, the INS Service began testing "screened in" refugees for HIV. The National Commission on AIDS estimated that the exclusionary provision kept out three to five hundred people per year.[304] Between 1991 and 1993, United States government ran a prison camp at Guantanamo Bay, filled with hundreds of Haitian refugees who allegedly tested positive for HIV.

A curious but formidable coalition of gay activists, immigration lawyers, African American and Haitian organizations, and students at various universities, formed around shutting down this Guantanamo prison camp, which had started under the Bush I administration. In the 1980s, the gay community was ravaged by the AIDS epidemic, at a time when no politician wanted to do anything about it. But to many AIDS activists, it was no longer acceptable to suffer in silence. As a result, AIDS activists came together to create AIDS Coalition to Unleash Power (ACT UP), a decentralized, grassroots network of advocates who believed that silence was equivalent to death, which fostered an urgent concern about ending discrimination against HIV-positive people.

Drawn to the battle against the HIV ban, activists from ACT UP conducted civil disobedience actions and dogged the new president, Bill Clinton, wherever he went, demanding that he shut down the camp and free the Haitian prisoners.[305] The changed political climate created by the organizing around the HIV prison camp at Guantanamo led District Court Judge Sterling Johnson Jr. to rule that the indefinite detention of HIV-positive asylum seekers without medical care was a blatant violation of constitutional due process.[306] The Clinton Administration did not appeal the decision, and instead, reached a settlement agreement to bring the Haitian refugees to the United States, and began using the camp at Guantanamo for other nefarious purposes.

However, President Clinton, who had campaigned on a promise to end the HIV ban, instead doubled down, and signed into law a ban on travel to the United States by persons with HIV.[307] Clinton similarly approved the Don't Ask, Don't Tell (DADT) policy, which allowed LGBT individuals to continue to serve in the military as long as they stayed in the closet, while also barring openly LBGT from joining the service.[308] The Clinton Administration also signed the DOMA into law, which prevented federal recognition of same-sex marriage.[309] These homophobic policies severely curtailed the civil rights of all LGBT citizens and immigrants.

ACT UP fell apart after internal division among the members about the direction of the organization. However, even though they were often dismissed as hysterical and too radical, ACT UP helped win the Ryan White Care Act, which in principle guarantees that nobody need die from AIDS merely because they cannot afford medications. After ACT UP disintegrated, the LGBT civil rights movement became more homogenous and reformist, focusing on making inroads with politicians, and prioritizing litigation as a means to victory. Despite persistent efforts from these LGBT advocates, the HIV ban would continue well into the Obama administration. In 2009, Congress passed legislation to eliminate the statutory HIV ban, which went into effect on January 4, 2010.[310]

The coalition that formed to end the use of Guantanamo as an HIV prison camp taught us one very valuable lesson—that it was possible to form a coalition without mandating that everyone agree on the same tactics as long as everyone had the same goal (in this case, shutting down Guantanamo). The groundwork had been laid for a new era of LGBT immigration advocacy.

Amos Lim

> **"If I was straight, I could get married. But I'm gay, and immigration law doesn't recognize my relationship."**
>
> —Amos Lim

After President Clinton signed the Defense of Marriage Act into law in 1996, LGBT advocates came up with a plan to ensure equal treatment for same-sex binational couples. Representative Jerrold Nadler, D-NY, introduced a bill to amend immigration policy to give same-sex partners of American citizens the same right to apply for citizenship as heterosexual spouses. Dubbed the Permanent Partners Immigration Act, and later the Uniting American Families Act (UAFA), the bill added "or permanent partner" wherever the word "spouse" appeared in the Immigration and Nationality Act.[311] This measure ensured that LGBT US citizens and lawful permanent residents would not have to pick between their love and their country, while it still continued to limit the legal definition of marriage to straight couples.

Championed by groups such as Immigration Equality (IE), the idea was far from radical or transformative. And yet, many mainstream immigration advocates balked at it, because they were tied up in the conservative politics of the church. They feared that efforts to include these reforms in a larger immigration reform bill would sink any chance of the bill's passage.

Amos Lim, a gay Singaporean activist, is one of many advocates who worked tirelessly on the issue. While growing up in Singapore, Lim dated girls who complained that he was "emotionally blocked off." Eventually, at age twenty-one he stopped dating girls, after falling in love with a man.

In 1995, Amos Lim met Michael Lim, his future spouse. They corresponded frequently and visited each other occasionally. In 1999, Amos Lim finally moved to the US to live with Michael. However, as a non-immigrant, Lim experienced the stress of an expiring student visa. He also saw how other same-sex, binational couples were being classified as "overstay risks" and unjustly denied entry to the United States. Over the years, Lim saw and heard from many people who were forced to leave the United States because the country did not allow them to live together here.

Being politicized to the intersection of queer and immigration justice issues, Lim realized how critical it was to create a grassroots organization for other couples in these situations. This led him and Michael to cofound Out4Immigration, a volunteer-led organization that empowered binational same-sex couples to share their stories.

As part of Out4Immigration, Lim made videos, circulated online petitions, wrote letters, op-eds, and blog posts and engaged with his local LGBT and immigrant rights communities to gain support for UAFA. Lim continued to maintain a non-immigrant visa as long as he could, though the chance that the UAFA legislation would pass faded with time.

Lim was instrumental in raising awareness of the unique struggles faced by same-sex binational couples and in bringing that into the larger immigration dialogue. In 2007, he organized San Francisco's Immigrant Rights Summit, where LGBT immigration issues were discussed for the first time. He was also part of the San Francisco City ID Card committee, which established municipal IDs for all individuals living in San Francisco, regardless of immigration status.

Lim's hopes were dashed in 2013 when Senators Schumer, Feinstein, Durbin, and Franken sided with eight Republicans to ensure that comprehensive immigration reform legislation did not include protections for the same-sex partners of US citizens and residents. (Even without those protections, the immigration reform legislation failed.) Fortunately, a month later, the United States Supreme Court struck down Section 3 of the DOMA, which had limited federal recognition of marriage to that between a man and a woman.[312] This made it possible for Lim and thousands like him to marry their partners and stay in the United States.

I was one of those thousands. My partner, Lindsay Schubiner, proposed to me the fateful day the Supreme Court struck down DOMA, and we married a couple months later, which ended deportation proceedings against me, and later granted me expedited citizenship.

Most post-industrial countries, such as Australia, New Zealand, Canada, and the European Union offer visas for permanent partners. In comparison, even though the United States now recognizes same-sex marriages, the Trump administration continues to try to take away immigration rights from those considered only domestic partners.[313]

Lim is now a United States citizen and lives in San Francisco with his spouse and child. For those interested in the thirty-six thousand binational couples who faced discrimination for many years, please see http://out4immigration.blogspot.com, where Lim has preserved hundreds of stories.

Tania Unzueta Carrasco

> "**We are not here to ask for acceptance. We are asking for change. We are asking for a chance to be able to contribute fully to our communities and our societies. We are asking for legalization... So undocumented brothers and sisters, let's come out and organize... Announce it over the speakers: *I am undocumented.*"**

—Tania Unzueta Carrasco

While scholars have only started to pay attention to how queer and immigration issues intersect, the history of conscious undocumented queer organizing goes back over twenty years.

Since 2001, the DREAM Act has been introduced in almost every session of Congress to provide a path to citizenship for undocumented students. The legislation was first introduced in 2001 by two Republicans, Senator Orrin Hatch (R-Utah) and Congressman Chris Cannon (R-Utah), and later adopted by Senator Richard Durbin (D-Illinois). The stated purpose of the DREAM Act was to "allow children who have been brought to the United States through no volition of their own the opportunity to fulfill their dreams, to secure a college degree and legal status."[314]

An estimated 1.7 million undocumented youth, 70,000 of whom graduate high school each year, face obstacles to higher education and to making a life for themselves in America. While the US Supreme Court had ruled in *Plyler v. Doe* (1981) that states could not ban undocumented children from attending public schools, no such provision existed for college-age undocumented adults who attended K–12 with the promise of *Plyler,* only to find that the doors to most higher education institutions were closed to them. Instead, after secondary school, most undocumented youth were confined to working in the same underground economy as their parents, thereby helping sustain a permanent underclass of workers.

One such undocumented youth, Tania Unzueta Carrasco, came forward to testify for a scheduled hearing on the DREAM Act on Capitol Hill in September 2001. At the time, Unzueta had just graduated from Lincoln Park High School in Chicago, Illinois, but even having been a swim team captain and with a 4.6 GPA, she could not attend college without a visa. At grave risk, she returned to her native Mexico to obtain a visa to lawfully attend college in the United States, but she was denied the visa because of her long overstay in the United States. Her family and community advocates quickly organized an effort to bring her back to the United States, and Senator Richard Durbin (IL) was able to secure her entry on a grant of humanitarian parole.

But the congressional hearing where Unzueta was supposed to testify was permanently postponed because of the attacks of September 11, 2001. The DREAM Act took a backseat to the war on terror, though Unzueta was ready to tell her story of growing up queer and undocumented in America. As time passed, mainstream immigration reform organizations held up passage of the DREAM Act by attaching it to a larger comprehensive immigration reform bill. This stagnation compelled the need for undocumented youth to start building their own networks. With the main argument for immigration reform being modeled on an appeal to traditional family values, many LGBT immigrant youth felt increasingly marginalized from the reform efforts.

Back in Pilsen, Chicago, during the push for immigration reform, Unzueta began organizing locally and served as a host for Radio Arte, an FM station affiliated with the Mexican Fine Arts Center Museum. She noted the hypocrisy of how the immigration reform movement focused on Elvira Arellano, an undocumented immigrant who took sanctuary in a church, but ignored Victoria Arellano, a transgender immigrant who died in detention when she was denied medication.[315]

When an undocumented Chicago student, Rigo Padilla, was detained by ICE in 2009 following a DUI arrest, Unzueta and other undocumented Chicago-area youth, such as Reyna Wences, organized locally to stop his deportation, which soon turned into a national campaign.[316] With the support of local and national community members and politicians, Padilla gained deferred action, and together, the three of them founded the Immigrant Youth Justice League (IYJL), to continue fighting for the federal DREAM Act.

In 2010, Unzueta and Wences, along with other immigrant youth and their allies from the IYJL, organized a "National Coming Out of the Shadows Day" and declared themselves "undocumented and unafraid." Borrowing from the LGBT leaders who came before them, this action brought much visibility to those who had been forced into two closets—the gay one and the undocumented one.

Two months later, in May 2010, Unzueta participated in the first sit-in at the late Senator John McCain's Arizona office, asking him to cosponsor the DREAM Act (which he had supported back in 2007). In July 2010, Unzueta and Wences were both arrested in the Senate Office building in DC while asking their Senators to do the same. The DREAM Act did not pass in 2010, but in pushing for a congressional vote, LGBT immigrants, such as Unzueta, gained mainstream attention for their cause. And perhaps more importantly, the growing visibility of queer undocumented youth activists led to a cultural transformation, where undocumented immigrants increasingly became unafraid to openly declare their immigration status, while also drawing the attention of their more mainstream LGBT counterparts.

Even after the fight for a standalone DREAM Act, Tania Unzueta Carrasco continued to organize nationally to end all deportations, and along with Marisa Franco, she spearheaded the #Not1More deportation campaign at the National Day Labor Organizing Network (NDLON). The campaign pressured President Obama to offer deferred action not just to undocumented youth, but also to the undocumented parents of US citizens.

Though she left NDLON, Unzueta continues to organize predominantly on behalf of those who were marginalized or left behind by the larger immigration reform movement in her capacity as the legal and policy director for Mijente, a national Latino organization that she helped to create in 2015. In her new role at Mijente, she has noted "before, we were happy with getting the win by telling the good story. Now I feel like the solution is: we build power, get leverage, and change culture."[317]

Unzueta has been at the forefront of immigration advocacy for almost twenty years now, and she is rarely given her due as the leader of a historic national movement, perhaps because she is queer or perhaps because she never seeks the spotlight, but instead focuses her efforts on elevating those around her.

It would be remiss to talk about Unzueta without mentioning her sister, Nadia Sol Ireri Unzueta, and her mother, Rosi Carrasco. Following in the footsteps of her elder sibling, Ireri

Unzueta organized and participated in various sit-ins to call attention to the detention and deportation regime. When she applied for deferred action under President Obama's DACA program, she was denied because of "civil disobedience, resisting arrest, obstruction of traffic, and reckless conduct."[318] Taking it in stride, and as many political dissenters have done before, she sued the Department of Homeland Security for retaliation for her political expression, and sure enough, they reversed their decision, granting her work authorization.[319]

Similarly, Rosi Carrasco continues to work and march alongside both her daughters against the criminalization of all people of color. Both Ireri Unzueta and Rosie Carrasco organize with Organized Communities Against Deportation (OCAD) in Chicago to stop the detention and deportation of local community members. The Unzueta siblings, their parents, and their friends were thrust into leadership roles by circumstances beyond their control, and they did not falter. They continue to be at the forefront of social change in their home city of Chicago.

Felipe Sousa Matos and Isabel Rodríguez

> "I don't care if I survive or not. Our people are disappearing. How many more until we've had enough? If there's any sacrifice I can make to keep from losing any more people, I will do it."

—Felipe Matos

Not all undocumented immigrant organizers were open about their sexual orientation from the beginning. In 2010, four young immigrants from Students Working for Equal Rights (SWER), two of them queer—Felipe Matos and Isabel Rodríguez—walked from Florida to Washington, DC as part of the "Trail of Dreams" to show the ongoing resistance against the criminalization of undocumented immigrants across the country. This campaign was intended to culminate on May 1, 2010, in Washington, DC with what would have been the first act of civil disobedience by undocumented leaders, but mainstream immigrant reform advocates convinced them not to take that risk.

That was not the only thing they were forbidden from doing. When Felipe Matos, a bisexual immigrant from Brazil, and his partner at the time, Isabel Rodríguez, a transgender woman from Colombia, participated in the Trail of Dreams, they had to keep their relationship secret out of fear of alienating conservative groups who supported their cause. At churches they were asked at times to sit separately. The support Matos and Rodríguez received from other undocumented youth across the country gave them the strength to be open about their relationship once they arrived in Washington, DC.

Matos was brought to the United States by his older sister when he was around fourteen years old. Growing up in Florida, to avoid "gay" thoughts, he tried to focus his energy on studies. Confused about his sexuality, Matos sought help in churches and other places, where he found constant rejection of him and his sexual orientation. He also had a difficult time obtaining higher education because Florida did not have in-state tuition. Matos hid his sexual orientation from even his employers out of fear that they would fire him.

Matos met Isabel Rodríguez through SWER, a Miami-based organization created in 2007 to push for comprehensive immigration legislation. Born in Bogota, Colombia, Rodríguez came to the United States at the age of six. Rodríguez gained lawful permanent resident status through a family petition in their teenage years.

Matos and Rodríguez started organizing together against the ongoing deportations, and soon joined talks with other immigration advocacy groups to create a national organization,

United We Dream (UWD). After several years of seeing no change, Matos and Rodríguez increasingly grew frustrated with the structures and methods of traditional advocacy organizations. For them, advocacy was not about attending meetings or writing grant applications, but about commitment and making sacrifices. They were inspired not only by the black civil rights and farmworker movements of yesteryears, but also by the youth resistance movement in Serbia (Otpor!), which had toppled the dictator Slobodan Milosevic.[320]

With little support from established immigration reform organizations, Matos and Rodríguez, along with their fellow Miami-Dade students Gaby Pacheco and Carlos Roa, set out on a 1,500 mile journey to walk from Florida to Washington, DC, on a national immigration pilgrimage. On their journey, they spoke to local community members, conducted workshops, shared their stories, confronted the Ku Klux Klan side-by-side with the NAACP, met with an anti-immigrant sheriff, and captured the hearts and minds of many more people.

Along the way, other advocates tried to co-opt the Trail of Dreams and use it to push for comprehensive immigration reform. They also tried to downplay that Matos or Rodríguez were queer and would benefit from legislation such as the "UAFA," a proposed bill to allow US citizens and lawful permanent residents to sponsor their permanent partners for immigration purposes. Many mainstream immigration reform advocates (Center for Community Change, National

Immigration Forum, America's Voice, Center for American Progress) virulently opposed the inclusion of UAFA in any comprehensive immigration reform measure because of their homophobia, and because the more conservative elements, such as the US Conference of Catholic Bishops, opposed granting equality to LGBT immigrants.

The Trail of Dreams walkers rose above the bickering and focused on communicating the urgency of immigration reform to the president. Finally, on June 28, 2010, Rodríguez, the only documented member of the group, was granted a meeting, along with other immigration reform advocates. Rodríguez noted that the president was both receptive and critical of the ideas and concerns brought forth.

While Matos, Rodríguez, and their friends are no longer at the forefront of the immigrant rights struggle, they continue to be involved in community and social justice work. After obtaining lawful permanent resident status through marriage to Rodríguez, Matos worked with United We Dream and the LGBTQ rights group GetEQUAL. He was also involved with the Contigo Fund, which raised money for the LGBTQ and Latinx communities after the Pulse nightclub shooting in Orlando, Florida. Matos now works at the Orlando Office of Multicultural Affairs as the LGBTQ Liaison. Rodríguez moved to New York for a graduate program at City University of New York, and she now works as a Program Officer at the Edward W. Hazen Foundation.

Matos, Rodríguez, and their friends who walked on the Trail of Dreams took a grave risk to come out of the shadows and organize at a time of rampant homophobia and transphobia, often in the same spaces that they inhabited. Their relentless pursuit of justice inspired many more to start their own journeys out of the shadows.

Mohammad Abdollahi

"If you organize, you are safe."

—Mohammad Abdollahi

Between 2005 and 2010, an increasing number of undocumented youth became active in local groups through the internet or by forming communities online. Many were initially reluctant to use their full names or show their faces, but nonetheless, they forged friendships, sometimes meeting up in person after enough trust had been established. These young people used the internet to bridge boundaries and form a community around a common cause and identity. Several undocumented students even started blogs to promote the federal DREAM Act. Others became active on forums such as the DREAM Act Portal (DAP), where they tried to organize. One of these individuals was Mohammad Abdollahi.

Now infamous in many immigration circles as a divisive figure of sorts, Abdollahi hailed from Iran, and came to the United States at the age of three. His parents were professors who were here on H-1 worker visas so Abdollahi maintained a visa until he aged out of H-4 dependent status at twenty-one. To this day, Abdollahi believes that part of why he was able to organize was because he was privileged in many ways; while growing up he had a social security number, a driver's license, and financial independence, which allowed him a level of freedom not available to many undocumented youth. However, the fact that he was gay made it very likely that he would be killed if he were ever deported to Iran.

Social media has increased the scale, velocity, and immediacy with which undocumented youth can connect, network, and organize locally. On the DAP forum that Abdollahi frequented before he was banned, he met other undocumented youth, such as Kemi Bello, Maria Marroquin, Mark Cortez, Juan Escalante, and me, who came together to form DreamActivist, an online network to push for passage of the federal DREAM Act.

In 2008, with the election of Barack Obama as president, Abdollahi spearheaded a social media push for the DREAM Act as one of the Top Ten Ideas for Change in America, at a time when no other immigration advocate was harnessing the power of social media in a similar way. Almost overnight, Abdollahi grew his tiny email list of supporters from a hundred to ten thousand. Suddenly many advocates started to pay attention to how undocumented youth were harnessing the power of social media to drive action.

Abdollahi was invited to assemblies of reform advocates and undocumented youth in Washington, DC, and New York that launched a national organization for undocumented students, United We Dream (UWD). After participating in its formation, Abdollahi soon realized that while it was important for undocumented youth to have a voice on Capitol Hill, the new organization was still under the control of the same old immigration reform advocates who did not seem interested in passing a standalone DREAM Act.

Indeed, funders and organizers from the Reform Immigration for America (RI4A) campaign, a multimillion-dollar effort, hoped to use the energy and actions of undocumented youth like Abdollahi to push for larger immigration reform. Frictions emerged between the undocumented youth, who saw a narrow window to once again push for the federal DREAM Act, and with the United We Dream network, now aligned with the RI4A campaign that wanted the "whole enchilada" of comprehensive immigration reform.

Abdollahi was driven by the urgency of organizing to stop the deportations of undocumented youth across the country, one case at a time. Between 2009 and 2012, by harnessing the power of social media and building local grassroots networks, Abdollahi and his team organized dozens of highly visible and successful campaigns targeted at the DHS to stop the deportations of undocumented youth.[321] Abdollahi was inspired by Harvey Milk and ACT UP, and constantly told his undocumented peers that they would be safer if they came out and organized.

New local groups, such as the IYJL in Chicago, DREAM Team Los Angeles (DTLA), and many others formed as a result of Abdollahi's inspiring local campaigns. These new undocumented youth-led organizations worked locally, while also engaging in national efforts to stop deportations in tandem with Abdollahi and other undocumented youth.

When the Trail of Dreams in May 2010 failed to call on Congress to pass a standalone DREAM Act, Abdollahi realized that they needed to take back control of the narrative. On May 17, 2010, four undocumented youth—Mohammad Abdollahi (Michigan), Yahaira Carrillo (Missouri), Tania Unzueta (Illinois), and Lizbeth Mateo (California)—along with an ally, Raul Alcaraz (Arizona), sat down in Senator John McCain's Tucson, Arizona office in the first known act of civil disobedience by undocumented immigrants, to demand a standalone federal DREAM Act.[322] Four of the five were queer, and together they helped to launch the fight for a standalone DREAM Act with The DREAM Is Coming campaign.

Abdollahi, Carrillo, and Mateo were arrested and released with a Notice to Appear in removal proceedings, which the government never filed in court. To try to quell their advocacy, the Obama administration also offered the four undocumented youth deferred action, but they refused to take the offer. However, because of Abdollhi's visibility, the Obama administration also targeted his family by placing his parents in removal proceedings. Tensions were high between him and his family because they blamed him for their situation, and Abdollahi had just come out to them as gay through the national news. Fortunately, his parents were later able to gain lawful permanent resident status through Abdollahi's younger US citizen sibling.

Three days after the McCain office sit-in, activists from DTLA shut down Wilshire Boulevard in Los Angeles in support of the DREAM Act. Undocumented youth in six different states launched a hunger strike, including one in Senator Chuck Schumer's (D-NY) office, in order to increase the sense of urgency for the standalone bill. In a subsequent action in July 2010 organized by Abdollahi, Carrillo, Unzueta, and Mateo, twenty-one undocumented students, eight of whom were queer, took over the US Capitol with the same demand for a standalone DREAM Act.

When the DREAM Act failed to garner enough votes to pass the Senate in December 2010, Abdollahi announced a split from United We Dream and the creation of the National Immigrant Youth Alliance (NIYA). Almost all undocumented youth chapters across the country joined the alliance and kept pressuring the administration to stop the deportations of undocumented youth.

NIYA activists took bolder and graver risks under Abdollahi's leadership, and infiltrated ICE detention facilities in several different states to bring attention to the plight of those facing deportations who had criminal records. In doing so, they highlighted more than their own stories, and started shifting the narrative of the immigration debate away from the "good immigrants" that the DREAM Act aimed to help, toward more abolitionist goals aimed at devastating the system of deportations.

Over time, because of a lack of resources and establishment support, and because of Abdollahi's top-down leadership style, many undocumented-led organizations either left NIYA or were kicked out by Abdollahi. After NIYA launched the bold "Bring Them Home" campaign in 2013, where several undocumented youth self-deported themselves to bring back other deportees from Mexico, Abdollahi became the target of several vindictive racist and homophobic personal attacks from liberal reform advocates who thought he had gone too far. While NIYA succeeded in bringing home dozens of previously deported individuals, including the infamous Elvira Arellano, the organization and Abdollahi himself were accused of trying to kill comprehensive immigration reform and of abusing the asylum process in order to achieve their goals.

Abdollahi is no longer at the forefront of immigrant rights organizing and prefers to work on campaigns only with a select few, where he keeps a low profile. He continues to hold "Secure Your Own Community" trainings designed to teach people and organizations how to fight deportations, and he now works on the "Sanctuary Collective"—a campaign led by undocumented people who are seeking sanctuary in churches from deportation orders. Regardless of what one might think of his highly disruptive tactics and leadership style, he succeeded many times in changing the national conversation on immigration, and he stopped the deportations of hundreds of individuals, at grave risk to himself and his family.

Abdollahi continues to be undocumented.

Yahaira Carrillo Rosales

"You don't wake up one day and say, 'This is a good day to get arrested.' We've been organizing for years. We've done everything else that we could, the faxing letters to Congress, the lobbying, the letter-writing campaigns, the conference panels, the media interviews. What else do we need to do for our political leaders to hear us?"

—Yahaira Carrillo Rosales

Yahaira Carrillo Rosales was born in Michoacán, Mexico, and crossed the border with her mother when she was eight years old. After residing for some time in Napa, California, Carrillo and her family moved to Kansas City, Missouri, which is where Carrillo spent the formative years of her childhood.

Carrillo's parents were migrant farm workers, but she did not let that dissuade her from pursuing higher education. In high school, Carrillo was part of the Reserve Officer Training Corps (ROTC) program, and she hoped to join the US Marines but could not do so without legal status. Due to her lack of immigration status, Carrillo also thought that she could not attend college. Her grades slipped, until she found out that she could take classes at a private university.

She enrolled in courses at Donnelly College in Kansas City, and later matriculated at Rockhurst University. In college she began to tell people about her queer identity. Her struggles as a queer immigrant propelled her to get more active in organizing for immigration reform. As a college student, she started to educate people about the DREAM Act and participated in a 2007 mock graduation in Washington, DC to illustrate the more than sixty-five thousand undocumented high school students who graduate each year and are shut out of higher education.

It took Carrillo eight years to finish her degree in Spanish Language and Literature at Rockhurst University, while she cleaned houses, translated, and performed odd jobs to raise money for college. As a student Carrillo started to organize to stop the deportations of her fellow students, and she cofounded the KSMODA DREAM Alliance. As part of the alliance, she joined national efforts to pass the DREAM Act, and also participated in the first known act of civil disobedience by undocumented youth when she sat down in Senator McCain's office in Arizona in May 2010, asking him to cosponsor the DREAM Act.

Carrillo thought that she would be deported after this action. In fact, everyone who had taken part in this action thought they would be detained, placed in removal proceedings, and deported to their home countries. But fortunately, Carrillo recounts that during her eight-hour detention at an ICE holding facility in Arizona, the toughest question she faced was what she wanted from McDonalds.

After her sit-in at Senator McCain's office, Carrillo found herself at the forefront of the immigrant youth debate. Along with her peers, she continued to organize for a standalone DREAM Act. Carrillo was also instrumental in bridging the divide between the DREAM Act and the LGBT movement's push for a repeal of DADT. Carrillo's inability to serve in the military was due to a two-fold discrimination: neither undocumented immigrants nor LGBT individuals could serve.

Other highly coordinated confrontational actions by undocumented youth leaders occurred around the same time that activists from GetEQUAL were employing similar tactics to achieve a repeal of the DADT policy. At one point, Carrillo notes how they had planned parallel actions in Washington, DC, which allowed arrestees to share the same court date and legal defense team to bail them out.

At Netroots Nation in July 2010, Carrillo met with Daniel Choi, who had just been discharged from the United States Army for being gay, after he came out publicly on *The Rachel Maddow Show*. At the time, Choi told Carrillo, "We might not have our documents, but we have our dreams." Therefore, even while harboring critiques of the military-industrial complex, Carrillo worked to build momentum for both DADT and the DREAM Act.

When the 2010 defense authorization bill came up for a vote, representatives from GetEQUAL and the undocumented youth movement collaborated to attach both the DREAM Act and DADT repeal to the larger military omnibus. The defense bill stalled in the Senate, and on December 18, 2010, the US Congress passed DADT, but failed to pass the DREAM Act.[323] However, Carrillo and her vocal efforts to build a more honest, inclusive movement laid the foundation for future collaboration between immigrant and LGBT groups.

It was not the end of the road for Carrillo. Because she was a survivor of a serious crime in the United States, Carrillo qualified for a lesser-known benefit, the U visa, which granted her lawful status with a pathway to citizenship. Carrillo became a lawful permanent resident in 2018, and around the same time, she also graduated with an MFA from Mills College. This time, because of her lawful status and steady job, it did not take her eight years.

Jorge Gutiérrez

> **"We are queer, we are trans, many of us might be undocumented, but we're organizing. Those most impacted can and should be on the front lines."**
>
> —Jorge Gutiérrez

Jorge Gutiérrez was born in Nayarit, Mexico. His family came to live in Santa Ana, California, when Jorge was ten years old.

One of the most defining incidents in his life happened when he was around sixteen years old. One day, while his mother, Amelia Cortez, was driving him somewhere, she turned to him and asked whether he liked girls. Gutiérrez almost lied because he was scared, but he admitted to her that he was gay. Coming out to his mother turned out to be a good decision, because she hugged him, and swore to protect him. Over time, Ms. Cortez became a vital ally in her son's journey as a queer undocumented leader.

California is one of the few states that provides in-state tuition to all students who attend three years of high school in the state, regardless of immigration status. Unlike undocumented students in many other states, Gutiérrez was therefore able to earn a Bachelor's in English from California State University, Fullerton. However, unable to actually use his degree, he was also drawn to passing the DREAM Act.

In 2010, Gutiérrez joined the Orange County DREAM Team. In July 2010, he participated in a fifteen-day hunger strike outside Senator Feinstein's office in California to gain her support for a standalone DREAM Act. In August 2010, along with DREAM Team LA and in collaboration with the Dream Is Coming, Gutiérrez helped organize the first DREAM Act town hall led by undocumented students for discussing the strategy and tactics of the movement. In September 2010, along with other undocumented youth leaders in California— Neidi Dominguez, Jonathan Pérez, and Nancy Meza—Gutiérrez penned a powerful piece in TruthOut, criticizing advocates in the non-profit world for making decisions about their lives without their involvement:

"The DREAM movement has come under criticism by liberal and conservative critics alike. We face racist, sexist, homophobic attacks from the right wing. From the left, many peace activists and immigration rights advocates disapprove of the DREAM Act because of its so-called military option. Meanwhile, CIRA supporters across the country remain largely silent in this debate and fail to heed the voices of undocumented youth activists."[324]

Along with Hector Plascencia and Marcos Nieves, Gutiérrez created the Queer Undocumented Collective with the goal of sharing lives, issues, and struggles of queer, undocumented immigrants to ensure that their voices were heard in the larger movement. Along with other queer undocumented youth, Gutiérrez pushed United We Dream to create space for queer immigrant youth at a time when such space did not exist on a national level.

Because of this pressure, in May 2012 United We Dream brought together sixty queer and undocumented leaders to launch the "Queer Undocumented Immigrant Project (QUIP)" to bring the LGBT and immigrant rights communities to the table in an intentional and strategic manner. Gutiérrez became the project coordinator of QUIP. He also cofounded DeColores Queer Orange County and the California Immigrant Youth Justice Alliance (CIYJA). Over time, Gutiérrez and QUIP were criticized for not being inclusive enough; in a later interview, an advocate noted that QUIP was dominated by queer Latinx men, and that queer women of color often felt excluded.

During the 2013 push for comprehensive immigration reform, Gutiérrez continued to encourage United We Dream and other organizations to include LGBT partners in the final legislation. He refused to pick one issue over the other. His efforts led to many mainstream LGBT organizations, such as the National Gay and Lesbian Task Force, GLAAD (originally the Gay and Lesbian Alliance Against Defamation), Lambda Legal, and the National Center for Lesbian Rights (NCLR) throwing their support behind a comprehensive immigration bill.

Over time, Gutiérrez grew more frustrated with how the Obama White House refused to meet and discuss immigration efforts with those who were directly impacted by immigration issues. After the 2013 immigration reform measure went down in flames, Gutiérrez left UWD and turned his attention to curbing the tide of deportations under the Obama administration.

Gutiérrez went on to work on issues related to transgender detention and now serves as the Executive Director of Familia: Trans Queer Liberation Movement, a national LGBTQ Latinx organization focused on working with transgender Latinx immigrants. In 2019, he brought together two hundred queer and transgender immigrants from across the country for a convention in Philadelphia, Pennsylvania.[325]

Through his past and present advocacy, Gutiérrez has ensured that undocuqueers are here to stay.

Julio Salgado

"I want to change the narrative for my people. That means creating art that does not put us in a perfect light, or a perfect immigrant narrative that only shows my good side. It's dangerous for us to show our flaws and so I hope that through my art, I can change that a little bit."

—Julio Salgado

One of the biggest criticisms of the DREAM Act and even DACA was that they created a dichotomy between good and bad immigrants. For years, when talking about immigration reform, advocates have cherry-picked and pushed to the forefront a few "aspiring American" undocumented youth—preferably those with perfect records, ideal people that they could splash on magazine covers, parade in front of journalists, or put on discussion panels. For some, this narrative of exceptionalism provided lawful status to a limited number of "ideal" immigrants while excluded millions who did not "measure up."

Julio Salgado, a queer undocumented "artivist," challenges this exceptionalism by doing something revolutionary: he depicts undocumented immigrants as completely average and incredibly messy. Born in Mexico in 1983, Julio Salgado immigrated to the United States with his parents when he was eleven years old. When his younger sister developed chronic kidney disease, requiring a kidney transplant from their mother, his family overstayed their visitor visas.

For more than a decade now, Salgado has traveled the country lecturing students, holding workshops, and speaking out about art, his immigration status, his queer identity, and his experience of living unapologetically.

As an artist, Salgado hustled his way through college and graduated with a degree in journalism from California State University, Long Beach. To challenge the narrative of exceptionalism, Salgado turned to video, writing, and graphic art to change how immigrants were depicted. He was also inspired by the work of other undocumented queer advocates, such as Abdollahi, Carrillo, and Unzueta, and he wanted to document the queer energy in the movement.

In 2010, Salgado cofounded the collaborative web project "Dreamers Adrift," along with Deisy Hernández, Fernando Romero, and Jesús Iñiguez, because as undocumented college graduates, they found themselves literally adrift without a future. While the website was originally created to encourage passage of the federal DREAM Act, by 2016 Dreamers Adrift had produced over ninety videos, including two web series: "Undocumented and Awkward" and "Osito."[326]

The Dreamers Adrift videos deconstructed the perfect model-citizen immigration lore that had been used as a safety crutch by so many. The videos depicted the very real and awkward lives of undocumented immigrants, from running into an old classmate while cleaning his hotel room, to not being able to enter a club for a date without an ID, to talking about sex, to taking jabs at hipsters for buying "undocumented" apparel that actual undocumented immigrants cannot afford. Far from depicting perfect, valedictorian, overachievers who just want to be American, Salgado depicted undocumented people as they exist, with their very real lives and struggles.

Prominent Oakland-based queer artist and advocate Favianna Rodríguez saw Selgado's art and offered to mentor him. Salgado took her up on her offer and moved to the San Francisco Bay Area, where he collaborated with her on many projects, as part of Culture Strike and co-taught a course at Stanford University on the intersection between visual art and social justice. Salgado also launched "I am UndocuQueer!"—an art project in conjunction with the Undocumented Queer Youth Collective, to highlight the presence of queer people in the movement. This culminated in 2013 in a giant "I am Undocuqueer" billboard by Galería de la Raza in San Francisco in honor of Pride month.

Salgado's trademark images are bright, cartoonish portraits of undocumented immigrants with political messages. His art prints also challenge the way in which the parents of undocumented youth are blamed for bringing them to the United States. In a powerful image of a Latinx family, Salgado wrote, "My parents are courageous and responsible. That's why I am here." His other posters had similar unapologetic statements, such as, "No longer interested in convincing you of my humanity, " and "Illegal faggots against borders."

Much like Unzueta, Salgado uses his craft to lift up the people around him. He has designed and shared on social media dozens of images to stop the deportations of undocumented immigrants. These images were shared by other advocates, printed, and placed in public places across the United States, and soon his artwork became synonymous with a movement.

Inspired by the late undocumented filmmaker Tam Tran, Salgado has turned to film as a way to shepherd cultural transformation. Salgado continues to create messy, complicated characters who do not fit into neat boxes or labels. Along with Jesús Iñiguez, he is currently working on a television pilot about a "homo-hetero" friendship in which the lead characters navigate the realities of being undocumented in a polarizing landscape.[327] Being his true authentic self is the only way that he can continue to thrive in these times as an undocuqueer artist and forge a new path forward for the rest of his peers.

People interested in purchasing Salgado's art prints can do so at http://juliosalgadoart.com.

José Antonio Vargas

"Home is not something I should have to earn."

—José Antonio Vargas

The most famous undocumented immigrant in the United States happens to be queer and Filipino, though he is often told to go back to Mexico.

A Pulitzer Prize winner, José Antonio Vargas came out as undocumented in June 2011 in his now well-known article, "My Life as an Undocumented Immigrant."[328] While Vargas has often expressed how the coming out strategies of LGBT activist and politician Harvey Milk inspired his own coming out as queer, it was the spaces created by queer undocumented youth that allowed him to publicly talk about his immigration status.

Vargas came to the United States by himself when he was twelve years old. His mother arranged for him to join his grandparents in Mountain View, California, and that's where he spent his teenage years. It wasn't his decision to come, but it has become his decision to stay in the United States. At the age of sixteen, while trying to obtain a driver's license with his fake Green Card and social security number, Vargas discovered that he was undocumented.

Vargas came out as gay to his grandparents in his teenage years because carrying one secret was hard enough. Vargas has said that his grandfather was upset when he came out as gay because, until the federal government recognized same-sex marriage, it closed off one possible pathway to citizenship.

Faced with an uncertain future, Vargas spent many years lying to get a job, trying to pass as American, and hiding that he was an immigrant, let alone an undocumented one. He worked at *The Washington Post*, where he won a Pulitzer in 2008 for his coverage of the Virginia Tech shooting. Vargas finally chose to come out because he was tired of hiding, though he did not realize that as the face of a hyper-critical movement, he would need at times to go further underground to hide his real politics and values.

Vargas came out as undocumented at a time when undocumented immigrant advocates were trying to get rid of the narrative of exceptionalism to include more people at the table when decisions were being made about their lives. While he was embraced by the same mainstream media that he had participated in for years, he was derided by many for becoming the face of a movement without having contributed to it during the years he was in hiding. Over the years, he has been called out for crossing picket lines, not sharing resources, not serving as a mentor to Asian American youth, for throwing his mother under the bus by blaming her for sending him to the United States, and has been accused of surrounding himself with white US citizens.

Nonetheless, he persisted, even as he pointed out that he was not trying to be an activist. Vargas created his own organization, Define American, and used it to try and change the narrative surrounding immigration, and to create media that advanced the conversation. In 2012, he successfully pushed the Associated Press and the *New York Times* to drop the term "illegal immigrant" in favor of "undocumented immigrant." He was left dejected and disappointed when, after he had spent many months of traveling the country and sharing his story, President Obama announced the DACA program, which gave temporary reprieve to those who would have qualified for the DREAM Act, because it did not cover Vargas himself. He had turned thirty-one years old just four months before the policy was announced, exceeding the age limits for the program by a fraction of a year.

Even though he failed to qualify for President Obama's DACA program, on the day before the DACA announcement Vargas shared space with other undocumented youth on the cover of *TIME Magazine*. Undeterred by an administration that had not tailored the program to meet his age, Vargas testified at a Senate Judiciary Committee hearing in February

2013 in support of immigration reform legislation. In 2014, while in McAllen, Texas for a UWD vigil, Vargas was arrested and detained by ICE, though he was never placed in removal proceedings.

Vargas has tried to share the media spotlight and extend his creativity beyond himself. He has established Define American chapters in colleges and universities across the United States, has collaborated with producers on media and television projects to showcase immigrants in a positive light, has released shorts and documentaries, and he continues to fund fellowships for undocumented artists.

Adrift without a home for many years, José Antonio Vargas earned a home in many hearts and minds. Last year he finally did buy a home for himself in Berkeley, California. A school in Mountain View, California, is named after him because of his courage and contributions to the movement.[329]

Lulú Martínez

Undocumented youth who organize act out of love for their families and communities when they put their bodies on the line to challenge nefarious, wrongheaded, and devastating immigration policies that continue to separate far too many loved ones. Lulú Martínez deserves to be recognized as someone who placed her life and future on hold to do what she felt was right: self-deport to Mexico to take part in the riskiest immigration action in United States history.

Lulú Martínez came to the United States at the age of three from Tlalnepantla, Mexico, and her family settled in Chicago, Illinois. She grew up in Portage Park and graduated from Payton College Prep in 2008. On March 10, 2010, in Chicago, along with Tania Unzueta, Martínez was one of many to come out as both queer and undocumented. A student at the University of Illinois in Chicago, Martínez joined the very risky nonviolent protest organized by NIYA—the Bring Them Home campaign.

Spearheaded by Mohammad Abdollahi and Lizbeth Mateo, the Bring Them Home campaign presented a different way of looking at immigration reform beyond the partisan vision of the Democrats and Republicans, whose debate about the pathway to citizenship had stalled the Comprehensive Immigration Reform (CIR) Act. Instead of handpicking which migrants would earn a pathway to citizenship according to respectability politics, Bring Them Home focused on the concept of belonging and on the simple idea that everyone had the right to live and work wherever they considered home. With the CIR Act stalled in the Senate, the campaign also wanted to highlight the record two million deportations under President Obama's administration.

Along with Marco Saavedra and Lizbeth Mateo, Martínez self-deported to Mexico and then attempted to come back to the border with a request for humanitarian parole, and asylum, and to bring with them other previously deported youth: Claudia Amaro, Mario Felix, Maria Ines Peniche, Luis Leon, Ceferino Santiago, and Adriana Gil Díaz.

The Bring Them Home campaign also had a second component. Martínez and her peers knew they would likely be detained after they presented themselves at the border. So they planned to organize in the detention center and collect stories of the injustices that their fellow detainees suffered while awaiting trial.

Martínez spent fifteen days in Eloy Detention Center, a for-profit facility notorious for its dire conditions. Eight of those days were in solitary confinement after she stood on a table and chanted "undocumented, unafraid," while handing out information about a legal helpline.[330] While she was at Eloy, NIYA and communities across the country mobilized support for Martínez and the other eight youth that had been detained in this action (known as the DREAM 9). They held rallies, pressured members of Congress to speak out in support, and publicized their stories. As a result, all nine were released from detention.

Martínez was acknowledged as a "Chicagoan of the Year" for her immigrant rights work. Even though she had been released,

Martínez was still in removal proceedings, and no longer qualified for DACA because she had left the country without authorization. Pressing ahead with her asylum claim, and represented by Aneesha Gandhi, an attorney who was a fellow LGBT immigrant, in 2018 Martínez won asylum.[331]

Many undocumented parents left their beloved homes and traveled long distances to give their children a safer home and hope for the future. Out of love for their children, they made the courageous, dangerous, and heartbreaking journey across many borders and oceans. Evoking a pathos of belonging, the Bring Them Home campaign attempted to reunite families in the United States. In many cases, they succeeded, and in many other cases, they took on too much, with too little.

Jennicet Eva Gutiérrez

> "There is no pride in how LGBTQ and transgender immigrants are treated in this country. If the president wants to celebrate with us, he should release the LGBTQ immigrants locked up in detention centers immediately."
>
> —Jennicet Gutiérrez

A black transgender woman, Marsha P. Johnson, threw the first brick at Stonewall, which sparked the modern LGBT civil rights movement.

Almost fifty years later, Jennicet Eva Gutiérrez a transgender woman and member of Familia: TQLM (Trans Queer Liberation Movement), did not need to cast a brick; her words were just as heavy.

In June 2015, Gutiérrez interrupted a White House reception where President Obama was delivering a speech about LGBTQ rights.[332] She told him to release all LGBTQ immigrants from ICE detention. As Obama attempted to cut her off, others in the crowd booed her and shouted, "This is not for you."

That incident does bring up an interesting question—for what and for whom are Pride celebrations at the White House held, at a time when transgender women and other LGBT people are caged, violated, and killed in detention facilities simply for trying to find a safe haven?

It is ironic that at a marriage equality celebration, Gutiérrez was treated similarly to the way marriage equality pioneer Anthony Sullivan was treated many decades before; people insinuated that she did not belong in the room, just as Sullivan had been told that he was fighting a losing battle.

Born in Mexico in 1986, Gutiérrez crossed the border at the age of fifteen to join her mother and eight siblings in the

San Fernando Valley, California. Gutiérrez came of age at a time when the immigration debate marginalized transgender women, and when the LGBTQ civil rights movement prioritized marriage equality at the expense of the survival of transgender people.

Gutiérrez was hardly the first immigrant to heckle Obama. As his deportation record grew worse over time, and after the abject failure of immigration reform, many advocates started to brand him the "Deporter-In-Chief." Advocates from the "Not One More Deportation" campaign protested outside detention facilities, chained themselves together to physically stop deportation buses, occupied the White House lawn with hunger strikes, and hounded Obama wherever he went. He was also criticized for creating "baby jails" and for detaining women and children together in deplorable conditions. Gutiérrez was just the first transgender woman to heckle him on transgender immigration issues.

The Monday after Gutiérrez interrupted Obama, ICE announced that transgender detainees would be housed in detention facilities that corresponded with their gender identity. The administration denied that the announcement had anything to do with Gutiérrez's bravery, but we all knew better.

DJ Sizzle Fantastic

"We have a whole country, we have a whole administration that sees us as targets, that sees us as the enemies, but we're not shriveling up. You may see us as that, but we see each other as greater beings that despite all of it, we're out here thriving. We're still out here living life, singing, dancing, and providing spaces where our communities can be themselves."

—Zacil Pech

Not all advocacy has to center around protesting and organizing militant movements. For many undocuqueers in the United States, the desire to live full lives in these turbulent times, regardless of immigration status, is very much part of the resistance. Born in Guerrero, Mexico, DJ Sizzle Fantastic or Zacil Pech, an undocumented DJ now residing in Boyle Heights, Los Angeles, embodies the drive to create music in times of crisis.

DJ Sizzle Fantastic migrated to the United States with her parents in search of a better life when she was only four years old. Growing up, Pech felt the pressure to assimilate and built a reputation as a cheerleader, while hiding that she worked as a food vendor and housekeeper to help her parents. However, when her undocumented status rendered her ineligible to become a cheerleading coach, she decided to speak up.

As a youth advocate, Pech organized with Defend Boyle Heights, an anti-gentrification campaign, organized with DREAM Team Los Angeles to push for passage of the federal DREAM Act, and later supported the #Not1More deportation campaign. In 2013 as part of an action targeting President Obama's record-breaking deportation machine, she was among several protesters who chained themselves to ladders to prevent buses with immigrants from leaving a federal detention facility. Pech also worked as the Health and Safety Organizer at The Garment Worker Center, an organization leading the anti-sweatshop movement to improve working conditions for garment workers in Los Angeles, most of whom were also undocumented.

A self-described "hell-raising *chingona*," Pech sought to create a safe haven to celebrate immigrants, while focusing on queer and women of color. She found that answer in queer Cumbia. Nowadays, she is the resident DJ for Chingona Fire, one of the largest Latina open mics in Los Angeles. She co-organizes #Cumbiatón (Boyle Heights / LA), an emerging Cumbia and Afro-Latinx party that pays homage to the *cultura* and *musica de barrios*, music that was an integral part of her upbringing.

To stay up to date with how DJ Sizzle is using music as a form of resistance and celebration, you can find her on Instagram

(http://www.instagram.com/sizzleo07) and SoundCloud
(http://soundcloud.com/djsizzle_007).

Conclusion

Over the course of queer immigration history, a significant
portion of the LGBT community and immigrants have been
placed outside of the law and denied equal protection. Queer
and gender non-conforming individuals were targeted, othered,
and excluded by the state as foreign threats. Undocumented
immigrants were regarded as especially undesirable. Together,
LGBT immigrants were undesirable twice over. And yet, in
the last decade, LGBT immigrants or "undocuqueers," as
some like to call themselves, became the driving force of a
historic movement.

Undocuqueers arose out of the marginalization of
undocumented immigrants from immigration spaces.
Young queer undocumented immigrants were done with
being welcomed only as immigrants, but not as queer or
transgender by an immigration lobby that was closely tied
to the conservative politics of the church. Many queer
immigrants also felt excluded from LGBT spaces, which were
predominantly white, cisgender, and US citizen-centric.
Therefore, queer and undocumented immigrant advocates
created and fostered their own spaces, which led to the

formation of grassroots organizations such as Southerners on the Ground (SONG), Familia: Trans Queer Liberation Movement, among many other safe spaces.

Even as the LGBT civil rights movement made great strides over the past decade, challenges remain. Regardless of immigration status, queer and transgender individuals face discrimination in the workplace, poor access to reproductive healthcare, homelessness, and criminalization. Transgender individuals continue to fight for the basic right to gender-neutral restrooms, fight for their place in the military, and transgender people of color face more hate violence than any other group in the United States. LGBT asylum seekers are subjected to traumatic ICE detention upon their arrival in the United States, in addition to the confusing asylum application process, which hardly anyone can navigate successfully without a competent attorney.

Countless other queer immigrants have taken part in this journey over the course of many years, too many to name, and they deserve a much longer chapter than can be included in this book. All of their lives merit thought and discussion and present the fundamental truth—we cannot expect to win the struggle for civil rights by failing to support one another.

THE NEW AGE OF RESISTANCE

. . . .

Thousands of immigrants in the United States woke up to a new political reality on November 9, 2016: Donald Trump, the most rabidly anti-immigrant, white supremacist politician in living memory, had ascended to the highest office in the country. Even in sanctuary cities with strong immigrant communities, people were visibly shaken, grieving, and fearful of what was to come. My own office was inundated with calls, emails, and drop-ins from undocumented young people and their parents, who were gripped with fear and uncertainty over what a president-elect Trump meant for their future.

During his election campaign, Trump promised to undo the reforms that so many immigrants had fought so hard to win. His plan for his first one hundred days in office included revoking the legal protections given to young immigrants through President Obama's DACA program, building a wall at the US-Mexico border, blocking funding for sanctuary cities, deporting people with criminal convictions, and making it harder to legally immigrate to the United States. Trump appointed hardliners to his transition team, such as

Kris Kobach, the architect of the anti-Muslim registration system (NSEERS), and Stephen Miller, who would become the architect of Trump's fervent anti-immigrant policies.

Trump moved quickly to put in place his anti-immigrant agenda. With Miller as his planner, Trump tried to end the DACA program, banned travel from predominantly Muslim countries, virtually eliminated refugee admissions, and began separating migrant children from their parents at the border to coerce them not coming to the United States. The attacks on immigrants, legal or not, seemed endless and relentless.

But throughout history, immigrants have shown that we can mobilize and resist under the gravest political circumstances. During the Bush administration, when Republicans introduced legislation to turn undocumented immigrants into felons, millions of demonstrators took to the streets in dozens of cities across the nation. The bill was defeated. Even as President Obama deported more than two million undocumented people between 2009 and 2016, immigrants came out as "undocumented and unafraid," and occupied streets, political offices, and lawns outside the White House and Congress.

The immigrants profiled in this chapter represent a tiny cross section of all who have led the resistance to Trump, but more importantly, their advocacy is not limited to mobilizing against Trump. Many immigrant organizers and advocates today came of age by surviving, organizing, resisting, and winning against draconian anti-immigrant laws. Their lives are testament that we can do it again.

Peter Schey

Few advocates are the subject of as much controversy as Peter Schey, who has been the President and Executive Director of the Center for Human Rights and Constitutional Law Foundation since 1980.

Schey's gentile parents fled the Holocaust, moving from France to England. Schey's father begged the United States to take in French Jews, but it ignored the request. The United States turned away thousands of French Jews, condemning them to be killed by Nazis who marched into France.[333] Eventually Schey's family moved to South Africa.

That was not a story that Schey or his parents told often, but it certainly inspired Schey to attempt what his father had been accomplish: ensure that no one trying to escape persecution or violence is left behind. Not one to turn the other cheek to injustice, a young Peter Schey started to take part in anti-apartheid protests in South Africa. The widespread government repression and violence in South Africa compelled his parents to move to the United States in 1962, when Schey was just fifteen years old. During the 1960s civil rights era, Schey attended University of California in Berkeley, and he was arrested during a Vietnam War protest.[334] He matriculated at California Western School of Law in San Diego and became a civil rights lawyer.

Schey has spent over four decades successfully suing the United States government in a myriad of cases. In the early 1980s, Schey received death threats for helping Haitian refugees who were seeking political asylum in the United States. He also served as counsel in *Plyler vs. Doe*, a landmark 1982 Supreme Court decision that allowed thousands of undocumented students the right to obtain a free public education in the United States.[335]

In the 1990s, Schey successfully sued to halt California's Proposition 187, an anti-immigrant initiative that prohibited undocumented immigrants from using non-emergency health care, public education, and other services.[336] In a series of complex cases, he also ensured that non-citizens are advised of their legal rights while they are detained.

One of his most famous cases involved the detention of migrant children, a critical topic in recent times. It began in 1985 with a call to Schey's office from a Hollywood actor requesting help for his maid's fifteen-year-old daughter, Jenny Flores, who had been caught while fleeing El Salvador's civil war, and was being detained in makeshift, unlicensed, and unsanitary conditions.[337] At the time, the United States was refusing to release unaccompanied minors to anyone other than their parents, and detained children were used as bait to capture undocumented parents living in the United States.

Along with his law associate at the time, Carlos Holguin, Peter Schey took the case and sued on behalf of Jenny Flores and the thousands of other unaccompanied minors detained in similar conditions. After a decade of litigation, in 1997 the United States government finally signed an agreement known as the Flores settlement, to keep children in less restrictive settings, create standards for the care and treatment of minors in detention, and to release minors to family or guardians without unreasonable delay.[338] The victory was short-lived, as Schey and others had to keep suing to improve conditions.

In many ways, we are back to where we started with respect to the Flores settlement agreement. In 2014, when Central American minors and their family members started to seek asylum in the United States in larger numbers, the Obama administration cracked down. DHS Secretary Jeh Johnson proclaimed, "We want to send a message that our border is not open to illegal migration; and if you come here, you should not expect to simply be released."[339] Secretary of State Hillary Clinton proclaimed, "Just because your child gets across the border, does not mean your child gets to stay."[340] In this manner, the Obama administration jailed the children and separated families in order to deter migrants who journeyed to the United States to seek asylum.

Upon taking office, Trump doubled down on this approach and used the arrival of asylum seekers to manufacture a national crisis, with the purpose of ending asylee protections altogether. The Trump administration started to separate children from their parents at the border as a way to deter migrants.[341] Many children were separated from their parents without any provision for reuniting them. Many children were kept in unlicensed, "black sites" without basic necessities.[342] Yet again, Schey found himself at the center of protecting the rights of unaccompanied minor children, though this time he had a legion of support from immigration lawyers across the country.

Despite his historic successes, Schey is hardly seen as a hero in the immigration world. Both conservatives and liberals have a litany of complaints about him. Conservatives complain that Schey has ruined the United States by enabling millions of undocumented immigrants to live here.[343] Liberals complain that Schey has made millions from filing lawsuits, and that he continues to neglectfully operate a shelter for homeless kids only to garner tax breaks.[344]

Whether the criticisms have any validity, Schey is undoubtedly an immigrant trailblazer, who has fought and won on behalf of immigrants in a long career of public service. Few advocates can claim his impressive line of victories against anti-immigrant laws. At a time when few immigration lawyers were immigrants themselves, Schey forged his own path forward, and in doing so, helped millions of immigrants live in the

United States. Now he is joined by many immigrant lawyers who continue to "make America great" but who also realize the limits of litigation.

Lizbeth Mateo-Jimenez

Lizbeth Mateo is one such attorney.

Many people know of Elvira Arellano, the immigration advocate who took sanctuary in a church in 2006 for a whole year and was deported shortly after she left the church.[345] But Lizbeth Mateo should be just as well known, because it was her advocacy that brought Elvira Arellano, and hundreds more, back to the United States after deportations.

Mateo migrated to the United States at the age of fourteen from a small town in Oaxaca, Mexico. In California, where legal residency is not a requirement for lawyers, Mateo works as an immigration and labor rights attorney. However, before she became a lawyer, Mateo was a community organizer.

> **"In 2008 I was knocking on doors to get President Obama elected, and now, in 2013, I will be knocking on America's door, asking President Obama to bring my community home."**
>
> —Lizbeth Mateo

Mateo started organizing undocumented students in 2006 and 2007 at Santa Monica College and California State, Northridge. She went on to join CHIRLA, a legal service provider that lobbied for immigration reform legislation, but she grew disillusioned with their strategy and approach and soon distanced herself from the organization. In 2010, Lizbeth Mateo sat down in Senator John McCain's office and risked deportation to Mexico in an effort to get support for the immediate passage of a standalone DREAM Act. In 2013, she sat down in Mayor Gray's office in Washington, DC to demand unmarked driver's licenses for all undocumented residents of the city. The same year, she voluntarily went back to Mexico as part of the Bring Them Home campaign and returned with eight others (including Marco Saavedra and Lulú Martínez) to seek asylum in the United States. Mateo and her compatriots were all detained at the border for over two weeks. Unpopular at the time, Mateo's very risky actions inspired hundreds of asylum seekers to do the same, including Elvira Arellano, who presented herself at the border and asked for asylum in 2014. Arellano and many of those who came back as part of the campaign were granted asylum status.

Mateo and her fellow organizers and their highly risky actions were blamed for trying to kill comprehensive immigration reform, and for the rise in unaccompanied minors seeking asylum in the United States (even though the general migration pattern has remained quite consistent over the past five years).[346] It is critical to note that at the time, Mateo and most undocumented immigrant rights organizers and grassroots organizations were completely at odds with immigration reform advocates, who pushed a top-down omnibus immigration reform bill (S. 744) in Washington, DC, and that Mateo and the others had plenty of criticisms of the legislation and of the strategy embraced by the reform campaign.[347]

During the fight for the DREAM Act, Mateo and her undocumented organizers pushed for a piecemeal approach in opposition the multimillion-dollar Reform Immigration For American (RI4A) campaign led by Frank Sharry at America's Voice, Ali Noorani at National Immigration Forum, Deepak Bhargava at Center for Community Change, and Angela Kelly at Center for American Progress, to name a few. Mateo and her team continued to push nationally for an end to the deportation of undocumented youth, a campaign that the reform advocates only supported when it was about to win. After the DACA announcement, Mateo kept pushing for the expansion of DACA for all, while also challenging the migrant detention complex, whereas reform advocates focused their efforts once again on passing inadequate legislation, this time disguised as the Alliance for Citizenship.

The continued failure of immigration reform legislation emboldened undocumented youth, who were tired of waiting for a piece of legislation to determine their fate.[348] In response, Mateo and her peers embarked on risky tactics such as civil disobedience, infiltrating detention camps, and even self-deportation as a way to push for administrative relief from President Obama, claiming that he had the discretion to expand upon DACA and to end migrant detention. The tactics of undocumented youth organizers were diametrically opposed to those advanced by immigration reform advocates, and both sides had scorn and derision for one another.

By using her relative privilege as a community organizer who would have qualified for DACA as a way to highlight the stories of humanitarian asylum seekers, Mateo inspired a new generation of organizers to think beyond immigration reform, demand more than DACA, and embrace transnational, cross-border organizing. Due to Mateo's highly visible cross-border organizing, many advocates, such as Pueblas Sin Fronteras and Al Otro Lado, now work with previously deported migrants or migrants trying to seek refuge in the United States.

In August 2013, Mateo was released from the detention facility after seventeen days, just in time to matriculate at Santa Clara University School of Law. Upon her graduation in 2016, Mateo revealed that the government had denied her application for DACA, because she had spent a couple weeks outside the country as part of the Bring Them Home campaign. Claiming that she was being punished for organizing the Bring Them Home campaign, over 250 professors, academic professionals, attorneys, and members of the community signed a letter asking the Obama administration to make an exception. They refused, sending the denial notice just a few days before Donald Trump took office so she could not respond in a timely manner. Mateo was left with a law degree that she could not use to work for any company or firm.

Mateo did not let the Obama administration's refusal to grant her DACA protection nor Trump's ascendancy to office deter her from continuing a life of advocacy. She opened her own law practice in Wilmington, California, a state that provides law licenses to all who have passed the bar exam, regardless of immigration status. In private practice, Mateo continues to represent the most vulnerable migrants. She was most recently thrust back into the spotlight for representing Edith Espinal, a migrant who is seeking sanctuary in a church as part of a new sanctuary movement. Espinal was fined $500,000 for not leaving the United States.[349] True to her character and strength, Mateo laughed when she saw the bill, and resolved to continue defending immigrants such as Espinal from the continued assaults by every political administration.

Mateo has only shifted her advocacy to lawful practice, but she is here to stay and embolden a new generation of undocumented lawyers and leaders.

The Infiltrators

During the Bring Them Home campaign, Mateo had the help of many highly spirited undocumented organizers. One of them was Marco Saavedra, who along with Claudia Muñoz, Jonathan Pérez, Felipe Baeza, Jesús Barrios, Sonia Guiñansaca, and Reyna Wences, infiltrated migrant detention centers to expose the conditions therein.

On July 11, 2012, Marco Saavedra, a citizen of Mexico living in the United States without legal authorization, went to the CBP office in Port Everglades, Florida and told the CBP officer that he was looking for his cousin who did not have a license and may have been arrested at a Border Protection checkpoint in the area.[350] He admitted to the CBP officer that he himself did not have papers to reside in the country and showed the officer an identification card from Mexico, stating that it was the only identification he could produce.[351] Upon further questioning, Saavedra told the CBP officer that he had entered the country with his cousin unlawfully when he was fifteen, through Arizona, and came to Fort Lauderdale in Florida, looking for work.[352] Due to Saavedra's purported lack of status, the CBP officer arrested and detained Saavedra at the Broward Transitional Center, a private immigration facility in Florida.[353]

The CBP officer didn't know that Marco Saavedra was an undocumented youth organizer with the NIYA, a national immigrant advocacy group of undocumented youth. Saavedra had come to the United States at the age of three with his parents in 1993 from Mexico. He graduated from Kenyon College, where he had pursued poetry and art, and served as a peer minister. Upon graduation, he worked at his family's restaurant, La Morada, a popular Oaxacan restaurant in the Bronx, New York.[354]

After taking part in dozens of civil disobedience actions, undocumented youth from NIYA learned that ICE under Obama did not want to detain them at demonstrations. Therefore, to expose the conditions at detention centers, they decided to go undercover. While Saavedra's infiltration of a detention center received widespread media coverage, including a feature by Ira Glass on This American Life, his infiltration was not the first, but it was the most successful of the attempts made by NIYA activists.

On November 10, 2011, Jonathan Pérez, a queer Afro-Colombian organizer from California, and Isaac Barrera from Boyle Heights, Los Angeles, went undercover and sought detention at the South Louisiana Correctional Center by presenting themselves as undocumented to the CBP office.[355] They were transferred to Basile Detention Center where they spent more than two weeks in custody before they were released. At Etowah County Detention Center in Alabama, four queer undocumented leaders—Felipe Baeza, Jesús Barrios Sonia Guiñansaca, Reyna Wences—were arrested and charged with criminal trespassing and disorderly conduct and incarcerated for two and a half days.[356]

In the next phase of attempted infiltrations, Saavedra traveled to Florida and presented himself to the CBP in the hopes that he would be detained and sent to the Broward Transitional Detention Center. Although the detention center in Broward has received the label of a "model facility" in the past, members of NIYA had received emails and letters from family members of detainees at Broward who had been locked up for months.[357] Once inside the detention center, NIYA organizers planned to work with other detainees, collect their stories and reveal how the Obama administration was detaining non-citizens who had committed no crimes or had convictions for minor crimes and was subjecting them to deportation.

Saavedra was joined inside the detention facility by Viridiana Martínez, a twenty-six-year-old undocumented woman, who founded the North Carolina DREAM Team, an immigrant youth group that advocated for the rights of undocumented youth in North Carolina.[358] For the next few weeks Saavedra and Martínez spoke with detainees and gathered information from them. NIYA set up a detention center hotline for detainees and/or their families to call in with details on each case. These details included the alien number, basic biographical information, contact information for the detainees' families and how they had ended up in detention.

By August 3, 2012, Saavedra and Martínez had collected and transmitted information on one hundred and ten individuals who should have been released from detention under the new guidelines issued by the Obama administration. Using the power of social media, thousands of emails were sent to ICE demanding their release. The organizing did not end there.

Inside the facility, Claudio Rojas started a hunger strike, which continued until he was released back to his family in Florida. Word of the conditions at Broward drew the attention and ire of twenty-six congressional representatives, who wrote a letter to ICE, demanding an investigation into detention practices at the facility.[359] NIYA organizers also occupied the political officers of Senator Bill Nelson (FL) to pressure him to support an investigation into the detention facility and call for the release of detainees.[360] Over the next few weeks, several dozen detainees were released.

Saavedra and Martínez themselves were released on August 4, 2012, and banned from coming back to the detention facility.[361] Their infiltration as undocumented immigrants and the response of the private prison to their activism demonstrated the power of undocumented youth organizing. In July 2013, Saavedra also joined Lizbeth Mateo and Lulú Martínez in self-deporting to Mexico, as part of the Bring Them Home campaign, to bring back those who had been deported from the United States.

Saavedra and Martínez are featured in *The Infiltrators*, a Cristina Ibarra and Alex Rivera movie that was showcased at Sundance in 2019.[362] Unfortunately on April 2, 2019, after the release of the documentary, ICE detained and deported Claudio Rojas, one of the detainees that Saavedra had helped to free, even after celebrities such as Ava DuVernay, John Leguizamo, and Laura Poitras signed letters to secure his release.[363] Rojas was likely targeted due to his own role in organizing hunger strikes inside the detention facility, and working with NIYA to obtain releases for other detainees. His detention and deportation are in line with the Trump administration's crackdown on immigration advocates.

After Saavedra and Martínez were released, NIYA continued these infiltrations to test whether the Obama administration was detaining and deporting only criminals, as it claimed. On April 4, 2013, Claudia Muñoz, an undocumented organizer from Monterrey, Mexico who grew up in Texas, infiltrated ICE in Michigan. Muñoz had no criminal record, but she was detained by CBP at the Ambassador Bridge to Canada. She was sent to Calhoun County Jail in Battle Creek, Michigan, where over the course of three weeks she exposed multiple human and civil rights violations.[364]

The Infiltrators continue to live almost normal lives in the United States. Only Claudia Muñoz continues to be in removal proceedings, and she also continues to be at the forefront of organizing to this day.

Angy Rivera

There was a time in United States history when women lost citizenship merely by marrying foreign-born men. Many single women were detained and deported at Ellis Island under the pretext that they could not possibly support themselves in the United States as anything other than sex workers—a ground of inadmissibility. Therefore, men dominated the immigrant labor workforce until after the sexual revolution. As more women were allowed into the United States and allowed to join the workforce, the face of immigration advocacy and organizing changed. Women immigrant rights leaders took center stage and started to speak openly about their own unique experiences of immigration.

Angy Rivera is one of the faces of this change. Born in Colombia in 1990, Rivera came to the United States in 1994 with her mother, Maria Rivera. They settled in New York, where Rivera grew up and continues to reside with her mother and four US citizen siblings. For much of her life, Rivera closely guarded two secrets. First, that she was the undocumented daughter of an undocumented mother. Second, that she had been sexually abused by her stepfather for four years.

Rivera was always involved in her community, but she stepped out of the shadows in her last year of high school when she heard about the federal DREAM Act, which could create a pathway to citizenship for undocumented young people such as herself. During college, Rivera interned with the New York State Youth Leadership Council (NYSYLC), an organization of undocumented youth.[365] At NYSYLC in 2010, she also started the first advice column for undocumented youth, Ask Angy, where she fielded questions on everything from driving without a license, to coping with trauma, to reporting domestic violence and assault.[366]

Through her advice column, Rivera rejected many notions that people take for granted about immigrants. She rejected the rhetoric that divided good immigrants from bad immigrants. She also spoke openly about how first-generation undocumented youth were forced to grow up too quickly and serve as parents to their own parents. Rivera also rejected the adage that migration was beautiful, a popular statement used by immigrant rights advocates:

"There is nothing beautiful about a mother or father having to leave their family behind to find work elsewhere...about immigrants dying while trying to cross the border into a country that still won't respect them...about people being raped, killed, or robbed while crossing the border... about people being raped, killed, or abused in detention centers..."

—Angy Rivera, critiquing Migration is Beautiful

As fate would have it, soon after President Obama announced the federal DACA program in 2012, Rivera went to a law center to apply for DACA. During a general legal screening, her attorney asked her whether she had been a victim of a crime in the United States, to which Rivera said yes and told the attorney about the sexual abuse she had endured at the hands of her stepfather. That is when she learned about the availability of the U visa that is granted to victims of serious crimes in the United States who can establish that they suffered physical or serious emotional harm from the incident and reported it to law enforcement.

She described how, even as a child, Rivera knew that what he was doing to her was wrong. She told her truth to her mother, who ensured that her partner would never hurt Rivera again. The younger Rivera testified against her perpetrator at trial, and her mother cooperated fully with social services to get her children back and protect them at all cost.

Rivera was shocked when she heard about the U visa, and her eligibility. She did not believe it, but she worked with the attorney to apply anyway. She did not need to do so but Rivera also stepped out of the shadows a second time by sharing her story of sexual abuse with the world online and became a vocal advocate for sexual assault survivors.

The U visa was created in 2001 as an incentive for vulnerable immigrants to report crimes against them. Rivera's personal account highlights how immigrants are particularly at risk of violence because of their unfamiliarity with their legal rights, misunderstanding of the US legal system, lack of access to service providers, and cultural and language barriers. Furthermore, after experiencing violence, the trauma, shame, and stigma combined with the lack of lawful status, creates a bigger barrier to reporting the violence and seeking help.

Rivera was one of the first women in undocumented spaces to address sexual assault and trauma and to speak openly about them. She wrote at length about sexual violence, toxic masculinity, how they impacted her life, and how they are pervasive in movement spaces. She also questioned the notion that she was a sexual assault survivor. Instead, she chose to call herself a warrior.

Rivera received her U visa in 2013 and became a lawful permanent resident in 2018. The entire experience was bittersweet, given that the United States was granting her lawful status not based on anything she had achieved or on her self-worth as a human being, but because of the severe childhood trauma she had endured. By chance, the filmmaker Mikaela Shwer read about Rivera's advice column in New York Magazine and contacted her. What was going to be a small video clip turned into a feature length documentary, No Le Digas a Nadie, which premiered as a PBS series in 2015 and won a Peabody award.[367]

But Rivera is not just defined by her trauma. Upon graduation from college, Rivera worked as a field coordinator for the National Latina Institute for Reproductive Health (NLIRH), an organization that fights for equal rights and access to reproductive health services. During her time there, Rivera evolved as a reproductive justice advocate, noting how it was nearly impossible for undocumented migrant women to seek reproductive services, especially in states without public transportation.

In 2018, Rivera was featured in a Maroon 5 video, "Girls Like You," as one of the many celebrities making a difference in the world.[368] We certainly need more women like Rivera, who continues to make a difference in the world, now as co-director of the NYSYLC, the same organization where she began her advocacy a decade ago. As the eldest child and a first-generation immigrant, Rivera also continues to take care of her mother and her younger siblings.

Erika Andiola

"A lot of us feel like we sort of shot ourselves in the foot. Because we stated the narrative like 'I was brought here by my parents, not my fault, poor me, I was here as a child' that kind of created blame on our parents."

—Erika Andiola

One of the most fervent and consistent critics of US immigration policies, Erika Andiola, began community organizing when she created the Arizona DREAM Act Coalition (ADAC) in Phoenix, Arizona, during an era when state and local anti-immigrant policies were gripping the nation.

In 2010, Arizona passed SB1070, a draconian law that legalized racial profiling by allowing law enforcement to arrest people based on reasonable suspicion that they were undocumented. As a key battleground state in the immigration fight, Arizona already had a history of anti-immigrant actions, ranging from Proposition 300, which banned financial benefits for undocumented students, to former Governor Janet

Napolitano sending the National Guard to the border, to the first state law in the nation prohibiting businesses from hiring undocumented immigrants.

Andiola's mother, Maria Guadalupe Arreola, fled to the United States from Mexico with five of her children, to escape poverty and domestic violence, and settled in California.[369] Andiola was eleven years old when she arrived in the United States. She picked up English quickly and became a star pupil, receiving scholarships from many colleges. But in 2006, Arizona voters passed Proposition 300, which prohibited in-state tuition for undocumented students, seriously jeopardizing Erika's chances to get a degree.

As a result, Andiola stared to organize locally and founded the ADAC to push for the passage of the federal DREAM Act. She was arrested as part of the first undocumented youth sit-in in Congress in July 2010. After the DREAM Act failed to pass, Andiola kept organizing locally and nationally with Dream (DRM) Action Coalition, alongside Cesar Vargas (the first openly undocumented attorney licensed in New York) and Celso Mireles. The DRM Action Coalition became the center of a court battle against the Senate filibuster rule, claiming that it had unfairly prevented the passage of the DREAM Act in 2010, which won a majority of votes in the Senate, but had failed to win the sixty needed to override a filibuster.[370] Unfortunately, the Supreme Court refused to hear the case. However, Andiola's efforts were rewarded on June 15, 2012, when President Obama announced the DACA program, which provided protection from deportations for DREAM Act eligible youth. However, the same protections did not extend to undocumented parents, which would continue to haunt Andiola.

Because of SB 1070, Andiola's own mother was profiled and pulled over in 2012 while driving in Mesa, Arizona, a few months after the DACA announcement.[371] Four months later, in January 2013, ICE arrested and detained Andiola's mother and brother while Andiola was at home.[372] Andiola went on overdrive to stop her family's imminent deportation, and asked advocates to call ICE to release her family.[373] Calls also poured in from Congress, because hours earlier, Andiola had been hired by Congressperson Kyrsten Sinema as an outreach director.[374] A day later, as Andiola's mother and brother sat in a bus headed to Mexico, the bus driver was told to turn the bus around. They were released and allowed to remain in the country. The directive to stop the bus most certainly came from Washington, DC.

When her mother and brother faced deportation, Andiola's advocacy helped transition the movement for the passage of the DREAM Act into a broader movement to stop deportations and family separation. After this harrowing experience, Andiola upped the ante and started to campaign fervently to stop deportations.

By June 2013, it became abundantly clear that an immigration reform bill that would have legalized millions and had passed the Senate, was dead on arrival in the House of Representatives. Andiola and many others, such as the Bring Them Home campaign, escalated their push to end all deportations as a down payment on immigration reform.[375] Andiola quit her position in Congress to participate in the #Not1More deportation campaign. In her new role, she could actively organize against deportations, especially now that the issue was personal: without an end to deportations, she could lose her mother and brother.[376] She started to organize full-time as part of DRM Action Coalition, and moved closer to Puente, a local group led by Carlos García that had been working on deportation issues for a long time.

As part of the #Not1More deportation campaign, in February 2014 Andiola and García started a hunger strike in Phoenix, Arizona to protest deportations.[377] At one point they were arrested and charged with trespassing, but Andiola took the show on the road, marching in the streets of Washington, DC and hunger striking on the White House lawn. Along with many undocumented advocates, Andiola signed onto a report calling on President Obama to expand deferred action to the fullest extent of the law, without specifying who should or should not benefit from this exercise of executive power.[378] In this manner, the immigrant rights movement evolved and embraced a narrative that did not rely on the politics of deserving and undeserving, but an ethos of keeping families together and ending family deportations.

Andiola continued her advocacy, joining the presidential campaign of Bernie Sanders in 2015, and lobbying the Vermont Senator on immigration issues. Even under the Trump administration, Andiola has continued to fight for a clean DREAM Act and organized against immigrant detention and deportations.[379] Given her personal struggles with immigration, Andiola is likely to remain at the forefront of immigrant rights advocacy for a long time. She currently works as the Chief Advocacy Officer for Refugee and Immigrant Center for Education and Legal Services (RAICES), the largest immigration legal services provider in Texas. As immigrant detention has increased in recent years, so has the importance of Andiola's advocacy.

Maru Mora-Villalpando

> **"We still fight. We resist. And we have been winning."**
>
> —Maru Mora-Villalpando

The United States runs the world's largest migrant detention system. It is a civil system wherein noncitizens are detained across the country in various types of facilities operated by the federal government or by private detention contractors, or in local jails. According to the most recently available statistics, US ICE detains over forty-two thousand people on any given day.[380] The growth of this civil detention system has continued unabated over the past two decades. Fortunately, due to the work of some advocates, such as Maru Mora-Villalpando, the United States is finally waking up to the inhumanity and indignity of putting migrants behind bars.

Maru Mora-Villalpando describes herself as a community organizer and mother. She entered the United States as a tourist from Mexico several times until 1996, when President Clinton signed into law the Illegal Immigration Reform and Immigrant Responsibility Act (IIRIRA). The legislation created dire consequences for people who overstayed their visas. Those who overstayed by six months but less than a year were subject to a three-year ban, while those who overstayed a year or more could not reenter until they spent ten years outside the country.[381] Perhaps no one anticipated that such a system would cage people inside the United States, and cause millions of undocumented immigrants to simply stay because leaving would mean never seeing their family members again.

Shortly after the laws changed in 1997, Villalpando found herself in this predicament after she gave birth to her US citizen daughter.[382] Villalpando realized that by overstaying her visa, she could no longer go back to Mexico and return as she usually did. Having a US citizen child complicated matters. Therefore, like many other undocumented and responsible parents, she made the choice to stay and raise her child in the United States, while trying to ascertain how she could legalize her status.

Villalpando went to many lawyers to discuss her immigration situation, and each time she was told to wait for the passage of comprehensive immigration reform. Eventually, she realized that she could no longer wait for legislation. She had to take her life into her own hands, so she shifted her focus from immigration reform to fighting against detention and deportations. Villalpando began to understand immigration reform as a lofty idea that Democrats used to gain votes and play lip service to immigrants, even while expanding the detention and deportation regime, only for it to end up in the hands of the Trump regime.[383]

To take control of her own destiny, Villalpando joined the Northwest Detention Center (NWDC) Resistance, a grassroots volunteer group working to end all detentions and deportations in Washington State. On a cold dreary morning in February 2014, as part of the #Not1More deportation campaign, Villalpando took part in a civil disobedience action to shut down Tacoma Detention Center, a private detention facility notorious for human rights violations.[384] Villalpando recalls the action as the one where she stopped being afraid because she finally realized that she was not alone:

"We were on the ground, five of us, sitting on the wet pavement, linked by PVC pipes in our arms. I became nervous and afraid of the arrests. But when the van stopped in front of us, I could see the driver's angry eyes. Immediately behind him, I saw hands, hands moving, and I realized those were the hands of people detained and shackled. I immediately told my compañeros: "Shout! *No están solos*! Shout with me!" And we shouted nonstop, chanting "no están solos!" We kept repeating this Spanish phrase, which means "you are not alone," until the van began to move backward and went back to the detention center."[385]

What came next was even more inspiring for Villalpando. Two weeks after the action, over 1,200 detainees at Tacoma Detention Center engaged in the largest ever hunger strike in a detention center, refusing meals in order to call attention to inhumane conditions inside the facility.[386] The first strike lasted fifty-six days, and led to many subsequent strikes that also spread to migrant detention centers in Texas and Oregon.[387] Villalpando realized that even as a free person, she should follow the lead of those who were detained and let them direct the work that she did on the outside. So she started to work on amplifying their stories, and focus more broadly on the needs of those who were in more vulnerable positions than herself.

Villalpando cofounded Mijente in July 2015, along with Tania Unzueta and Marisa Franco, to create a space that was not just pro-Latinx, but also pro-queer, pro-woman, pro-black, and more. Advocates at Mijente have been at the forefront of organizing with groups such as Black Lives Matter to address police violence, racial profiling, and gang databases, because these issues intersect and impact all our communities. At Mijente, advocates are disrupting constructions of deservingness by organizing around those who are ordinarily seen as less deserving and are labeled as criminals.

Alas, Villalpando's activism and increasing visibility made her a target for ICE. In December 2017, she received a Notice to Appear in removal proceedings after ICE learned of her activism through a newspaper article.[388] In an interview, she says she laughed when she received the letter because she knew that the Trump administration was trying to send her a message to stop her political activism.[389] It confirmed that what she was doing was important and threatened this anti-immigrant administration enough for them to single her out. Even while in removal proceedings, Villalpando continued to organize, and she attended the 2018 State of the Union as a guest of Senator Maria Cantwell (D-WA).[390]

However, by the time ICE started removal proceedings against her, Villalpando's US citizen daughter was about to turn twenty-one, the age at which a US citizen child can finally sponsor their parent for immigration s status. Therefore, an immigration judge granted Villalpando a continuance to allow her to gain status through her US citizen daughter.

Jonathan Jayes-Green

Led by African Americans, the 1960s movement for civil rights called for the end of all forms of racial discrimination. This did not impact only African Americans but led to a widespread transformation in US migration policy as President Lyndon Johnson moved to end the racially discriminatory quota system that had severely banned or restricted immigration from all countries except from Western Europe.[391] The 1965 Immigration and Nationality Act abolished the national origins quotas that had barred nearly all Asian and African newcomers. The Act established a preference framework centered on family unity, skilled migration, and refugee admission, and continues to be the foundation of the present-day legal immigration system in the United States.

Despite these advancements in civil rights and immigration policy, black non-citizens disproportionally suffer the brunt of immigration enforcement efforts. Although only seven percent of non-citizens are black, they make up more than ten percent of the population in removal proceedings and constitute twenty percent of deportations based on criminal grounds.[392] As the number of black immigrants grew in the United States, so did the links between law enforcement, the criminal justice system, prisons, and the migrant detention and deportation complex.

In response to anti-immigrant efforts to create laws that criminalize migration, advocates have for years paradoxically declared that immigrants are not criminals. However, this position, while well-intentioned, also leaves behind those who have previously committed crimes, and those who have been racially profiled by the criminal justice system. Hence, efforts to pass immigration reform by portraying immigrants as good and deserving excludes an entire group of immigrants who have been unfairly profiled, detained, and targeted by a racist criminal justice system, and then cast aside for removal. Therefore, the narrative that immigrants are not criminals ignores and perpetuates the very real criminalization that black immigrants undergo in the United States.

Many undocumented and black leaders have been vocal about the fact that they have historically faced the harms of both the criminal justice system and immigration enforcement but remain on the margins of the immigration debate. One of them is Jonathan Jayes-Green. Born in Panama, Jayes-Green and his family came to the United States searching for the elusive American dream when he was thirteen years old. They came on tourist visas but overstayed, leaving a young Jayes-Green undocumented and without legal recourse. Jayes-Green excelled in high school and, despite facing many barriers to higher education because of his lack of legal status, earned a bachelor's degree in sociology from Goucher College. He applied for and received DACA in March 2013, which allowed him to officially join the workforce.

Jayes-Green served as liaison to and advocate of the Caribbean and Latinx communities in the office of the Governor of Maryland, after winning state-wide legislative fights like the Maryland DREAM Act and marriage equality. However, over time, he noticed and felt the very real marginalization that black immigrants undergo in immigrant rights spaces. He also felt hurt and distraught that the immigrant community that he was so much a part of did not stand with the Black Lives Matter movement to protest the violence against black people.[393] Needing a place to heal, share resources, and talk to people undergoing similar struggles, he cofounded the UndocuBlack Network (UBN), a multigenerational network of black undocumented immigrants. UBN focuses on organizing, deportation defense, advocacy, wellness, and storytelling.

Jayes-Green is vocal about the fact that even though he is not undocumented, he is likely to be stopped by law enforcement for merely driving or walking and could end up as a statistic in the criminal justice system. From there, he remarks "it is a fast track to deportation."[394]

> "Anti-blackness has played a role in the mainstream immigrant rights movement. Black immigrants are detained and deported at five times the rate of their presence in the undocumented immigrant community. Due to our identities, our communities are more likely to be targeted for enforcement, criminalization, and deportation in this country—and that has to stop"
>
> —Jonathan Jayes-Green

Through the UndocuBlack network, Jayes-Green and his peers regularly organize on issues that intersect with black lives, such as getting black migrant asylum seekers released from detention. UBN has also led the way to protect immigration relief programs that predominantly impact black immigrants, such as Temporary Protected Status (TPS) and Deferred Enforced Departure (DED). TPS is a temporary legal status granted to non-citizens who are endangered by conditions in their home country, such as ongoing armed conflict, environmental disaster, epidemic, or other extraordinary events. DED is a humanitarian program authorized under the president's power to conduct foreign relations. Sudan, Somalia, Haiti, and Liberia are some of the countries that in the past have received TPS and DED designations. They have enabled foreign citizens from those countries to continue to live and work here till the crises in their home countries can be averted or resolved.

In many cases, the designations have lasted for more than a decade, leading people to build entire lives in the United States without a designated pathway to lawful permanent resident status. There are currently approximately 437,000 people with TPS in the United States from ten designated countries: El Salvador, Haiti, Honduras, Nepal, Nicaragua, Somalia, Sudan, South Sudan, Syria, and Yemen. People from Liberia have been granted DED.[395] Many of these designated countries continue to be besieged by conflict, disasters, and epidemics.

Despite this, the Trump administration on March 31, 2019 threw many TPS recipients into turmoil by refusing to recertify their designations and attempted to end DED for Liberia. On behalf of UBN, several organizations filed a lawsuit against the administration for its decision to terminate the DED program for Liberia.[396] On April 11, 2019, UBN won a temporary victory when a federal district court judge set aside the termination of TPS for Haiti, citing racial bias.[397] However, while UBN had won a battle, the struggle is ongoing to keep and eventually extend or make these programs permanent.

As with the central theme of the undocumented immigrant movement today, Jayes-Green believes freedom and liberation is possible by organizing and focusing on the voices and leadership of those directly impacted. And Jayes-Green is certainly among those who are directly impacted and are leading us toward a more inclusive and just world.

Barnali Ghosh

To create a more just world, immigrants cannot focus on just winning immigrant rights, but also on issues that impact us more broadly. Many immigrant trailblazers do not limit their activism to just immigration issues, but also pursue broader social justice issues, such as reproductive health, criminal justice, and environmental justice. Quite often, these issues intersect with one another.

Barnali Ghosh lives in Berkeley, California, and she organizes locally, but thinks globally. Ghosh was born in 1974 in Kolkata, West Bengal, and grew up in Bengaluru (Bangalore, Karnataka). She completed her undergraduate degree in architecture in India, and she moved to the United States on a student visa in 1999 to go to graduate school at UC Berkeley. There, she met her future husband, Anirvan Chatterjee, an immigrant from Canada. With roots in Bangalore, India, Ghosh is always thinking about what she can do to make things better, not just in her local community, but also in Bangalore.

As a landscape artist, Ghosh has designed parks, playgrounds, and streetscapes across the state, and works in the intersection of cities, climate, and activism. Ghosh is an environmental justice advocate at heart, and she spent a year interviewing over sixty climate activists in twelve countries, as part of the Year of No Flying project. She now does transit, walking, and biking advocacy as the Vice Chair of the Transportation Committee for the City of Berkeley, California, while also spearheading many community projects.

As part of Brown and Green, a loose network that includes teachers and engineers, Ghosh and others have marched, rallied, and joined activists from across the Bay Area in Richmond, California, fighting to reduce pollution from the large Chevron refinery.[398]Ghosh believes that politicians have for too long passed on the responsibility for climate matters to the consumer, while the real villains, such as oil companies are actually in our backyard, and to get rid of them, we need to tackle them locally.

Ghosh and Chatterjee are also community-based historians who have spent decades collecting and archiving the oral history of South Asian immigrants. They run the Berkeley South Asian Radical History Walking Tour, where they use a two-mile course to share radical South Asian immigrant history in order to inspire new activism and to pass on their collective knowledge to future activists. The tour specifically shares stories of people with roots in South Asia, including those from Pakistan, India, Bangladesh, Sri Lanka, Nepal, Bhutan, and Afghanistan.

The walking tour includes an anecdote about Ali Ishtiaq, a gay Bangladeshi man and the creator of Trikone, the first queer group focused on South Asians. The proceeds of the tour are given to community projects and help fund Bay Area Solidarity Summer (BASS), a five-day leadership program for South Asian youth. By collecting, archiving, and sharing the almost lost history of trailblazers, both Ghosh and Chatterjee over time have become trailblazers themselves.

Therese Patricia Okoumou

"When they go low, we go high. And I went as high as I could."

—Therese Patricia Okoumou

Former First Lady Michelle Obama certainly did not mean for anyone to climb the Statue of Liberty when she told people of color to act graciously in the face of the racism directed at us. But Therese Patricia Okoumou took it quite literally.

Therese Patricia Okoumou is an immigrant from the Republic of Congo who lives in Staten Island, New York. She arrived in the United States on August 2, 1994, with a visitor visa and overstayed it. She eventually did gain US citizenship. In 2017, after losing her job, Okoumou became a member of Rise and Resist, a New York-based direct action group committed to opposing, disrupting, and defeating any government actions that threaten democracy, equality, and civil liberties. She had been working as personal trainer and put that training to good use by scaling great heights in support of migrant children. On July 4, 2018, forty-five-year-old Therese Patricia Okoumou climbed the Statue of Liberty to protest the Trump administration's "zero tolerance" immigration policy that had caused thousands of migrant children to be separated from their parents.[399]

Along with Okoumou, seven members of Rise and Resist were arrested for hanging a large banner reading "Abolish ICE" on the statue's pedestal. During a standoff with a cop while she was huddled on the statue, millions of viewers tuned in to watch. Okoumou recounts that she thought he would shoot her, and told the cop that her life "doesn't matter to me now, what matters to me is that in a democracy we are holding children in cages."[400] Okoumou was arrested and charged with trespassing, interference with government agency functions, and disorderly conduct.

Okoumou did not stop there. She kept climbing higher. In December 2018, despite facing a prison sentence, she went to Paris, France, climbed halfway up the Eiffel Tower, and unfurled a banner that read #ReturnTheChildren, before she was forcibly removed by police.[401] These actions reflected the infuriation felt by many advocates who for months had watched in dismay and horror as the Trump administration unlawfully separated migrant children from their parents at the border, and then lost track of them.[402] Investigative reporters uncovered that after being separated from their parents, migrant children were sent to unlicensed black sites, and kept in overcrowded concentration camps, under squalid conditions, deprived of proper nutrition and essentials such as toothbrushes.

In continued protest of Trump immigration policies, in February 2019 Okoumou traveled through Texas on a ten-day journey, where she visited several detention centers, and at one site climbed a fence to wish the children a Happy Valentine's Day. Okoumou also climbed the Southwest Key building in Austin, Texas, in February 2019 to protest for-profit prisons for immigrant children, and occupied it for over eight hours. This action violated the terms of her bail, and she was placed under house arrest with an ankle bracelet.

On March 19, 2019, Okoumou went to criminal court for her sentencing hearing with tape over her mouth. The judge asked her to remove it, and she complied. Okoumou was sentenced to five years of probation and two hundred hours of community service.[403] Nonetheless, she resolved to continue climbing buildings in protest of injustices.

Okoumou insisted on continuing her civil disobedience actions because the United States was openly committing even greater atrocities, such as tear-gassing migrant children and their parents.[404] Okoumou is just one of many who have started to call for abolishing ICE, the agency responsible for arresting and detaining non-citizens.

During the Bush and Obama years, immigrant rights trailblazers fought for rights that placed them at odds with both the government and mainstream groups that touted the forever failed comprehensive immigration reform omnibus legislation. Their highly spirited actions made them constant targets of criticism.

As immigration advocates, we live in times of infinite crisis, with the Trump administration regularly rolling out a new cruel plan to detain and deport immigrants. As President of the United States, Trump has taken steps to roll back all protections that had been put into place for undocumented youth, has banned Muslims from lawfully immigrating, inflicted trauma on unaccompanied migrant children in order to coerce their parents, promoted indefinite detention, increased prosecutions for illegal reentry, eliminated refugee admissions, and expanded the system of expedited removals, among many other anti-immigrant measures.

Yet this administration has faced strong challenges every step of the way, because of advocacy from immigration lawyers, undocumented youth, parents, and detainees at the federal, state, and local level. The strong advocacy of undocumented youth such as Angy Rivera, undocumented parents such as Maru Mora-Villalpando, and undocumented attorneys such as

Lizbeth Mateo with respect to leading their own struggle has pushed advocates to sit up and pay attention to those who are directly impacted by the immigration policies.

This chapter contains just a small cross section of immigrant rights activism today. Because of their own advocacy, and because of programs such as deferred action, many immigrant rights community organizers and advocates were able to enter professions previously shut to them. Non-citizens such as Juan Escalante at FWD.us, Ainee Athar at Chan Zuckerbeg Foundation, Anthony Ng at Advancing Justice in Los Angeles, Sonia Guiñansaca at CultureStrike, Claudia Muñoz at Grassroots Leadership, and Reyna Montoya at Aliento, Arizona are now some of the drivers of non-profit immigration advocacy. Many more migrants continue to be shut out of spheres of professional work, but they continue to pave the way forward. Along with the trailblazers covered in this chapter, they continue to be the face of modern-day resistance to anti-immigrant laws.

AFTERWORD

• • • • • • • • • • • •

Winston Churchill once remarked wryly that history is written by the victors. Perhaps it was a rather cynical dismissal of those who had fought and lost, those who were easily erased or dismissed from the hegemonic narrative of history. Or perhaps, Churchill was right, and by authoring this historical account of trailblazing immigrants, I know that we have been victorious.

Migration is as old as human history. Most migrants endure tremendous trauma and hardship in leaving everything they know, journey on many dangerous paths to make their way to another country seeking freedom, opportunity, and a fresh start. Most of us try our hardest to follow the law, find a way to legalize, to support our family members, and give back to the community that gave us a new home. The migrants profiled in this book are just a few of the many people who have faced significant obstacles on their way to living a complete and full life, and "nonetheless, persisted." As people who have taken a chance, and exposed ourselves to grave risk in the United States, we do not deserve condemnation. We deserve respect because we are making America the great place that it can be for everyone.

Most often, migration is a byproduct of capitalism. Through foreign military intervention, and neoliberal policies, the United States has created conditions that force people to flee their homes, and then once they arrive at our shores, it has scapegoated these same people for economic woes beyond their control. The United States demarcates the bodies of non-citizens as either immigrants or non-immigrants, legal or illegal. Most of us try to come here lawfully, and after failing to do so, enter without papers out of desperation, not out of disregard for the law. Many of us change from one visa status to another, and sometimes fall out of status, becoming permanently alienated from the country where we live and work. In many parts of the world, due to the actions of the United States, there is no longer a home for many of us to go back to.

More than ever before, migrants are being locked out of pathways to lawful permanent residence and citizenship, and face a growing apparatus of detention and deportation. While legalization does not guarantee freedom or liberation from the state apparatus, it does provide some stability, and protects people from deportation (most of the time). Therefore, throughout history, the foreign-born have fought to expand the notion of citizenship, and along with it, the notion of who belongs in the United States. Perhaps it is time to question the concept of citizenship and why it should be the arbiter of rights. Human rights should not be so arbitrary that they cease to exist simply because one crosses a geopolitical border in search for freedom or opportunity.

Trailblazers, though, do not just wait patiently to be granted rights. They do not hang out in long lines and waiting rooms. They do not wait for despotic regimes to find and kill them, and they certainly do not bend in the face of authoritarian leadership. They organize protests, campaign against deportations, sue the government, hold sit-ins in political offices, infiltrate detention centers, create art, write poetry, and vote with their feet. In these ways, immigrants throughout history have taken part in mass civic participation, even in places that disenfranchise them.

Many migrant advocates know that regardless of who is in office, we will need to resist local and national immigration enforcement against all marginalized communities. Under President Obama, we had to fight our liberal friends to win temporary relief from deportations. As horrible as Trump is for immigrants, there is little doubt that a Clinton presidency would have likely brought other types of draconian enforcement and without half of the outrage.

No matter who is in power, we need to shift away from purely electoral politics to mobilize and protect our communities. For far too long, migrants have been used as a political football to elect politicians who simply perpetuate the issues that lead to migration in the first place. Therefore, support for politicians should be the least of our concerns as a community. We need to engage all people who are left behind by the political establishment. Our strength as a community lies in our values. And our values should be defined not by those who want to take America back to the dark ages, but by those who want it open to all.

At the same time, there is no shame in simply surviving and going about our day without engaging in the political process. Migrants are shamed for leaving our countries. We are derided for coming here. We are embarrassed for working low-wage jobs that no one else wants, and envied for the high-wage jobs that no one else can do. We are blamed for not leaving when things get hard. We are subjected to jeers for wanting to leave to build a life elsewhere and for leaving toxic organizing spaces and workspaces. But there is no shame in taking care of ourselves and putting ourselves and our families first.

The tragedies of detention and deportation are not new. These issues have long existed. As the stories in this book shows, under every political administration, people from all ages, races, ethnicities, spiritual association, genders, sexual orientations, and socioeconomic status have fought long and hard for their right to live freely in the United States. Our voices have been stripped, stifled, and unheard, and our bodies marginalized, castigated, and erased quite often from our own history.

And yet, there are people waiting and wanting to engage with these issues, and they are mostly well-intentioned. However, the onus of integrating these energized people cannot be on the existing advocates and organizers, who are already burned out from resisting. People who want to truly contribute to the struggle for migrant rights must take the initiative to educate themselves, read, use the internet as a tool, and meet organizers halfway, wherever they are, at any given moment. Donate to organizations that are on the ground, attend know-your-rights trainings, talk to family, friends, and neighbors about the issue, get involved locally with a volunteer group to promote sanctuary city policies, and so on.

We cannot just fight the federal and state anti-immigrant policies that Trump and those who follow him will continue to promote. Litigation is just one tool in our arsenal, and critical to beating back the onslaught of anti-immigrant measures put forth by Trump, but it is not the way to commandeer social change. Now is the time to imagine what we can do differently. We need to be on the offensive and reimagine a different world, whether it is a world without deportations, without detention camps, or a world without draconian immigration enforcement.

We need to bring forward pro-immigrant measures through local and state legislation, as well as continue to organize for education, universal healthcare, an actual social safety net, and for better environmental policies. As Trump launches an onslaught against our sanctuary cities, we need to push to end cooperation between local police and immigration enforcement. As Trump revokes legal protections for young immigrants, we need to ensure our K–12 and higher education institutions continue to be safe spaces for our students. We need to take to the streets with migrants proclaiming they won't go back into the shadows, while at the same time pursuing creative litigation strategies for more permanent relief for all migrants. We need to make our city and local governments actual sanctuary zones. With lawyers, advocates, and community members, we need to resist all deportations with every tool at our disposal.

We need to think nationally and engage locally. Most of all, we must continue to be bold and uncompromising in our vision of justice. And under every political administration, we need to continue to take our cues from those who are directly impacted by nefarious policies, and follow their lead.

Finally, as migrants, we overcompensate a lot simply because we still feel like we do not belong. We are told to feel grateful for what we have been given and leave the country if we have valid criticisms about how to make it better. Many of us come bearing the gift of food, language, culture, and yet work hard to unlearn these gifts. Some of us condemn our peers for their sharp tongues, criticisms of the United States, for how they may be perceived, and for how their actions and words can be misused and misconstrued by those in power. Some of us care too much about fitting into perfect little boxes, and try to sanitize our lives, and make our stories ready for consumption as part of a narrative of immigrant exceptionalism.

We get it wrong. Trying to assimilate, unlearning our accents, hiding our orientations, and touting our achievements will not change the minds of those who do not want us here. As the people profiled in this book have established time and again, we ought to be unafraid and unapologetic and forge our own paths forward.

After all, that is what trailblazers do.

ACKNOWLEDGMENTS

• • • • • • • • • • •

This book would not be possible without my hard-working and brilliant parents, Usha and Pradeep Lal, who brought me to the United States when I was a child, despite my many protests and misgivings, which continued late into adulthood. I am grateful to live in a place where I can live my best life, while also working so everyone else can also.

I am grateful to all my rabble-rousing undocumented and formerly undocumented friends who have made history, and continue to make a history that I am privileged enough to write. Special gratitude to Claudia Muñoz Castellano, My Le, Adriana Ramos, super-sisters Claudia and Brenda Amaro, for their support and overwhelming love no matter where I am and what I am doing.

My partner, Lindsay Schubiner, put up with me talking about this book for longer than it took me to write it. Thank you for your endless love, patience and for providing valuable feedback.

I'm not sure if I should acknowledge Rosie, my poodle mix, because she can't even read this but she was present for the writing of every word of this book since she follows me everywhere.

The cover was designed by undocumented artivist Julio Salgado, who told me a long time ago that he would draw the cover to my book if I ever wrote one. And he did. Great follow-through.

I have known Professor Allegra McLeod, the forewordist for this book, for over a decade, long before I was even a law student, and she continues to be an inspiration, intellectual force in legal academia, and a role model for her students at Georgetown Law. Thank you.

There is no way I would have written this book if it was not for Hugo Villabona and the whole team at Mango Publishing, who had faith in my ability to pen something of value, and provided valuable feedback at every turn. It has been a wonderful journey from start to finish, and almost unbelievable.

Finally, I would like to thank all my teachers and professors for sharing their wisdom and knowledge, and for putting up with my endless questioning of authority.

SUGGESTED CONTRIBUTIONS

· · · · · · · · · · · ·

There are hundreds of organizations working to help migrants in the United States, and many are local charities, legal and advocacy non-profits. Many are well-funded by both public and private dollars. Here is a non-exhaustive list of the smaller grassroots non-profits working on cutting-edge immigration issues, whose work is often unsung and who deserve your support:

ALDEA PJC | PRO BONO IMMIGRATION LEGAL SERVICES:

Aldea PJC is a 501(c)(3) nonprofit organization based in Reading, PA, that protects the rights of underserved immigrant children, families, and other refugees, by providing all with access to high-quality, pro bono legal representation. https://aldeapjc.org/donate

BLACK ALLIANCE FOR JUST IMMIGRATION (BAJI): BAJI

educates and engages African American and black immigrant communities to organize and advocate for racial, social and economic justice.
https://blackalliance.com

BLACK LGBTQIA+ MIGRANT PROJECT (BLMP): Housed at Transgender Law Center, BLMP was created to address the ways in which the Black community is targeted by the criminal law and immigration enforcement system, and marginalized in the broader migrant community, and racial and economic justice movements.
https://transgenderlawcenter.org/programs/blmp

BORDER ANGELS: The organization provides dozens of water jugs along "high-traffic migrant paths" in the desert, free and low-cost legal aid in English and Spanish every week at the San Diego-based Sherman Height Community Center.
https://www.borderangels.org

CALIFORNIA IMMIGRANT YOUTH JUSTICE ALLIANCE (CIYJA): CIYJA is a statewide immigrant youth-led alliance that focuses on placing immigrant youth in advocacy and policy delegations in order to ensure pro-immigrant policies go beyond legalization, and shed light on how the criminalization of immigrants varies based on identity.
https://ciyja.org/

CULTURE-STRIKE: CultureStrike empowers immigrant artists to dream big, disrupt the status quo, and envision a truly just world rooted in shared humanity.
https://www.culturestrike.org/donate

EL/LA PARA TRANS LATINAS: El/La is an organization for transgender Latinas (translatinas) that works to build collective vision and action to promote our survival and improve our quality of life in the San Francisco Bay Area.
http://ellaparatranslatinas.yolasite.com/

FAMILIA: TRANS QUEER LIBERATION MOVEMENT: A national organization that addresses, organizes, educates, and advocates for the issues most important to our lesbian, gay, bisexual, transgender, and queer (LGBTQ) and Latino communities.
https://familiatqlm.org

FREE MIGRATION PROJECT: This organization represents immigrant clients in legal proceedings, provides legal support and training to organizers and advocates, engages in public education and outreach, litigates in the public interest, and advocates for fair and open immigration laws.
https://freemigrationproject.org/

JUNTOS: A community-led non-profit organization that works to fight for the rights of Latinx-immigrant community in Philadelphia.
http://vamosjuntos.org/

JUST FUTURES LAW: Our movement needs unapologetically abolitionist lawyers to work with grassroots advocates to advance change. Just Futures Law is a women of color led, transformative immigration law project rooted in movement

lawyering.
http://justfutureslaw.org/

KOREATOWN POPULAR ASSEMBLY: Organized neighbors and
workers in Koreatown, Los Angeles who have organically built
a strong and organized community to push back against ICE
and deportations.
http://paypal.me/KtownPopularAssembly

MIJENTE: If you support an immigrant rights movement that
is pro-Black, pro-indigena, pro-worker, pro-mujer, pro-LGBTQ
and pro-migrant, you should give your money to the people at
the frontlines of the struggle at Mijente.
https://members.mijente.net/donate

MOVIMIENTO COSECHA – THE SEED PROJECT: Born out of the
pain and uncertainty of the repeal of DACA, the Seed Project is
a nonviolent organization fighting for permanent protection for
undocumented youth.
https://www.lahuelga.com/

QUEER DETAINEE EMPOWERMENT PROJECT (QDEP): A post-
release support, detention center visitation, direct service,
and community organizing project that works with LGBTQ
immigrant prisoners and their families currently in detention
centers in New York, New Jersey and Connecticut.
http://www.qdep.org/donate/

PUEBLO SIN FRONTERAS: The group behind the refugee and migrant caravans, Pueblo Sin Fronteras is a trans-border organization made up of human rights defenders who help migrants stay together to protect themselves from danger on their way to the United States.
https://www.pueblosinfronteras.org/

UNDOCUBLACK NETWORK: A multi-generational network of currently and formerly undocumented Black people that fosters community, facilitates access to resources, and contributes to transforming the realities of Black people.
https://undocublack.org/

WESTERN STATES CENTER: Based in the Pacific Northwest and Mountain States, Western States Center works nationwide to battle white nationalism so that all people can live, love, and work free from fear.
https://www.westernstatescenter.org/

GLOSSARY

. . . .

Since the immigration system can appear complex and convoluted with plenty of jargon, this is a glossary of terms to help make the system more understandable.

ALIEN: A legal term referring to any person who is not a citizen of the United States. We prefer to use the term noncitizen, to refer to anyone who is not a citizen or national of the United States.

ADMISSION: Any noncitizen seeking to gain entry into the United States at a port of entry by going through official channels is deemed to be seeking admission to the United States.

ADJUSTMENT OF STATUS (AOS): Process whereby noncitizens already in the United States seek to change their immigration status to lawful permanent resident (a.k.a., a Green Card holder).

AGGRAVATED FELONY: Any criminal conviction that falls within a long list of categories defined in the Immigration and Nationality Act.

ASYLEE: A person granted asylum after coming to the United States.

DACA: Program created by the Obama administration in 2012 to give temporary two-year work permits to undocumented youth between the ages of fifteen and thirty-one, who had come to the United States before they turned sixteen, and lived in the United States since June 15, 2007, and did not have more than three misdemeanors.

DEFERRED ACTION: An act of discretion on the part of the DHS to not deport a non-citizen without lawful status. An individual who has received deferred action is authorized by DHS to be present in the United States, and is therefore considered by DHS to be lawfully present (see definition below), but not have lawful status.

DETAINER: A request from ICE that a law enforcement agency should maintain custody of a non-citizen who would otherwise be released to provide ICE time to assume custody of the non-citizen.

DEPORTABLE: When a non-citizen has been admitted to the United States and is subject to one of the many grounds for deportation, including overstaying a visa.

CITIZEN OR USC: A person who has the right—through birth or naturalization—to live in the United States permanently without being subject to immigration law.

CONVICTION: A criminal disposition that is broader in the immigration context and may include expunged convictions, deferred adjudications, and judgments not regarded as convictions under state law.

CRIME INVOLVING MORAL TURPITUDE: A category of crimes, including theft and fraud that involve some sort of "evil intent" or are deemed contrary to contemporary social mores. A conviction for a crime involving moral turpitude can make any non-citizen deportable.

EXPEDITED REMOVAL: This is a process by which a non-US citizen can be denied entry and physically removed from the United States at a port of entry or within one hundred miles of the border without being admitted. Usually, this occurs in cases where the intending immigrant is deemed to not possess a valid entry document or commits fraud or misrepresentation.

EWI (ENTRY WITHOUT INSPECTION): A non-citizen who enters the US without being lawfully admitted.

FUGITIVE ALIEN: An individual with an unexecuted order of removal.

GOOD MORAL CHARACTER: When one has committed no criminal acts that would provide evidence for lack of good moral character.

IMMIGRANT: Legally, this term refers to a lawful permanent resident or Green Card holder, though it has been used more broadly to describe everyone who was not born in the United States or a US territory or possession.

INADMISSIBILITY: A non-citizen can be deemed to not qualify for admission to the United States based on numerable factors, such as communicable disease, criminal background, terrorism, and security reasons.

LAWFUL PRESENCE: Any non-citizen who resides in the US with official permission, i.e. an unexpired visa or deferred action status, is deemed to be lawfully present.

NATIONAL: Certain persons born in outlying territories of the US who are not subject to removal from the United States.

NATURALIZATION: Process by which a lawful permanent resident applies for and becomes a US citizen.

NON-IMMIGRANT: A non-citizen who seeks entry to the US on a temporary basis for a specific purpose.

OVERSTAY: A non-immigrant whose visa has expired, or who has had her visa revoked after violating its conditions.

REFUGEE: A person eligible to receive asylum and, generally, granted asylum outside the United States.

RETURN: The non-judicial process of returning a noncitizen who is deemed inadmissible or deportable from the United States to their country of origin, where there is no formal order of removal issued by a judge.

REMOVAL: This is a formal order to leave the country issued after the conclusion of immigration court proceedings. A non-citizen who is removable and is removed is ineligible to immigrate to the United States for at least ten years and subject to criminal penalties if s/he reenters without authorization.

TEMPORARY PROTECTED STATUS (TPS): A non-citizen protected from removal because her country is designated on a list of countries suffering from natural disasters or political strife.

UNDOCUMENTED OR UNAUTHORIZED: An informal term to describe noncitizens who have no legal authorization to remain in the United States.

UNLAWFUL PRESENCE: A non-citizen who does not have lawful nonimmigrant status and who is not in the period of authorized stay, such as deferred action, is generally unlawfully present in the United States. Accruing more than a year of unlawful presence in the US as an adult, bars an individual from admission to the United States for ten years.

VISA WAIVER PROGRAM: A program that allows noncitizens from certain designated countries to enter the United States temporarily without a visa.

VOLUNTARY DEPARTURE: When an individual agrees to depart the United States, and is generally given 120 days to do so, as opposed to a deportation.

VOLUNTARY RETURN: When an individual is caught trying to enter the country and agrees to voluntarily return instead of undergoing expedited removal.

WORKSITE ENFORCEMENT ACTION: violent, sloppy raids of workplaces that puts US companies out of business and workers out of jobs.

SOURCES

• • • • • • • • • • •

1 Sherwood, Henry N. "Early Negro Deportation Projects." *Journal of American History*, Volume 2, Issue 4, 1 March 1916, Pages 484–508, doi.org/10.2307/1886908.

2 Rashid, Kamau. "Slavery of the Mind: Carter G. Woodson and Jacob H. Carruthers-Intergenerational Discourse on African Education and Social Change." *Western Journal of Black Studies*, vol. 29, no. 1, 2005, pp. 542–546. *ProQuest*, proxygwa.wrlc.org/login?url=https://search-proquest-com.proxygwa.wrlc.org/docview/200338355?accountid=33473.

3 Kates, Don B. "Abolition, Deportation, Integration: Attitudes Toward Slavery in the Early Republic." *The Journal of Negro History*, vol. 53, no. 1, 1968, pp. 33–47. *JSTOR*, www.jstor.org/stable/2716389.

4 Kates, Don B. "Abolition, Deportation, Integration: Attitudes Toward Slavery in the Early Republic." *The Journal of Negro History*, vol. 53, no. 1, 1968, pp. 33–47. *JSTOR*, www.jstor.org/stable/2716389.

5   Finnie, Gordon E. "The Antislavery Movement in the Upper South Before 1840."*The Journal of Southern History*, vol. 35, no. 3, 1969, pp. 319–342.*JSTOR*, www.jstor.org/stable/2205761.

6   Rogers, J. A. "ROGERS SAYS: LINCOLN WANTED TO DEPORT NEGROES, AND OPPOSED EQUAL RIGHTS." *The Pittsburgh Courier (1911–1950)*, Feb 26, 1944, pp. 7. *ProQuest*, proxygwa.wrlc.org/login?url=https://search-proquest-com.proxygwa.wrlc.org/docview/202158795?accountid=33473.

7   Act March 26, 1790, c. 3, 1 Stat. 103.

8   *Scott v. Sandford*, 60 U.S. 393, 399 (1857).

9   Merelli, Annalisa, and Annalisa Merelli. "A History of American Anti-Immigrant Bias, Starting with Ben Franklin's Hatred of Germans." *Quartz*, 12 Feb. 2017, qz.com/904933/a-history-of-american-anti-immigrant-bias-starting-with-benjamin-franklins-hatred-of-the-germans/.

10   Norton, Sydney. "German Immigrant Abolitionists: Fighting For a Free Missouri." *Saint Louis University Deutschheim State Historic Site,* 2016, hermanndeutschheimverein.org/images/abolitionists_exhibit_catalog.pdf

11   Ibid.

12   Ibid.

13   Ibid.

14   Abrams, Kerry. "The Hidden Dimension of Nineteenth-Century Immigration Law." Vanderbilt Law Review 62 (2009).

15   George Anthony Peffer, *If They Don't Bring Their Women Here: Chinese Female Immigration Before Exclusion*, 9 (1999).

16   Chinese Exclusion Act, ch. 126, 22 Stat. 58 (1882), repealed, Act of Dec. 17, 1943, ch. 344, 57 Stat. 600.

17   *United States v. Wong Kim Ark*, 169 U.S. 649 (1898).

18   Siegel, Robert. "He Famously Fought For His U.S. Citizenship. Where Are His Descendants Now?" *NPR*, 2 Oct. 2015, www.npr.org/2015/10/02/445346769/he-famously-fought-for-his-u-s-citizenship-where-are-his-descendants-now.

19   Act of December 17, 1943, "An Act to Repeal the Chinese Exclusion Acts, to Establish Quotas, and for Other Purposes." (57 Stat. 600; 8 U.S.C. 212a).

20   Act of Oct. 1, 1888, ch. 1064, 25 Stat. 504.

21   Act of May 5, 1892, ch. 60, 27 Stat. 25 (1892)
      ("Geary Act").

22   Regulations Governing the Registration and
      Fingerprinting of Aliens in Accordance with the Alien
      Registration Act, 1940, 5 Fed. Reg. 2,836, 2,838 (Aug.
      14, 1940).

23   Taylor Hansen, Lawrence D. "The Chinese Six
      Companies of San Francisco and the Smuggling of
      Chinese Immigrants Across the U.S.-Mexico Border,
      1882–1930."*Journal of the Southwest*, vol. 48, no.
      1, 2006, pp. 37–61. ProQuest, proxygwa.wrlc.org/
      login?url=https://search-proquest-com.proxygwa.wrlc.
      org/docview/210891734?accountid=33473.

24   H.R. Rep. No. 53–70, at 1 (1893).

25   *Fong Yue Ting v. United States*, 149 U.S. 698 (1893).

26   *Japanese Immigrant Case*, 189 U.S. 86 (1903).

27   Moloney, Deirdre M. "National Insecurities: Immigrants
      and U.S. Deportation Policy Since 1882." Chapel Hill:
      University of North Carolina Press (2012).

28   Gómez, Sonia C. "Why Women Have Become Targets
      in the Immigration Fight." *The Washington Post*, WP
      Company, 22 Mar. 2019, www.washingtonpost.com/

outlook/2019/03/22/why-women-have-become-targets-immigration-fight/.

29   Lakhani, Nina. "This Is What the Hours after Being Deported Look Like." *The Guardian*, Guardian News and Media, 12 Dec. 2017, www.theguardian.com/inequality/2017/dec/12/mexico-deportation-tijuana-trump-border.

30   Fernández, Manny. "'You Have to Pay With Your Body': The Hidden Nightmare of Sexual Violence on the Border." *The New York Times*, 3 Mar. 2019, www.nytimes.com/2019/03/03/us/border-rapes-migrant-women.html.

31   Fix, Michael E., editor. *Immigrants and Welfare: The Impact of Welfare Reform on America's Newcomers*. Russell Sage Foundation, 2009. JSTOR, www.jstor.org/stable/10.7758/9781610446228.

32   CONG. GLOBE, 41st Cong., 2d Sess. 5121 (1870).

33   *In re Halladjian*, 174 F. 834, 844 (1909).

34   Carbado, Devon W. "Yellow by Law." 97 *California Law Review* 633–92 (2009).

35   *Ozawa v. United States*, 260 U.S. 178 (1922).

36   Coulson, Doug. "British Imperialism, the Indian Independence Movement, and the Racial Eligibility

Provisions of the Naturalization Act: United States v.
Thind Revisited." *Georgetown Journal of Law & Modern
Critical Race Perspectives* 7 (2015): 1–42.

37   Lal, Vinay. *VI: Exile in the New Canaan.* The Other
Indians. Harper Collins, 2012.

38   Bailey, Thomas A. "California, Japan, and the Alien
Land Legislation of 1913." *Pacific Historical Review,*
vol. 1, no. 1, 1932, pp. 36–59. JSTOR, www.jstor.org/
stable/3633745.

39   Cuison Villazor, Rose. "Rediscovering Oyama v.
California: At the Intersection of Property, Race, and
Citizenship." Washington University Law Review 7, no. 5
(2010): 979–1042.

40   Ferguson, Edwin E. "The California Alien Land Law and
the Fourteenth Amendment." California Law Review
35 (1947).

41   McGovney, Dudley O. "The Anti-Japanese Land Laws of
California and Ten Other States." Calif. L. Rev. 7 (1947).

42   *Oyama v. California,* 332 U.S. 633, 635 (1948); *Fujii v.
California,* 242 P.2d 617 (Cal. 1952)

43   Reft, Ryan. "Courting Division: How Three Southern
California Court Cases Bolstered and Hindered
Multiracial Civil Rights Movements." *KCET,* 1 Jan.

2017, www.kcet.org/history-society/courting-division-how-three-southern-california-court-cases-bolstered-and-hindered.

44 *People v. Oyama*, 29 Cal. 2d 164, 167 (1946).

45 *Oyama v. California*, 332 U.S. 633, 635 (1948);

46 Cuison Villazor, Rose. "Rediscovering Oyama v. California: At the Intersection of Property, Race, and Citizenship." Washington University Law Review 7, no. 5 (2010): 979–1042.

47 "Sei Fujii v. State of California." *The American Journal of International Law*, vol. 46, no. 3, 1952, pp. 559–573. JSTOR, www.jstor.org/stable/2194519.

48 Civil Liberties Act of 1988, 50 U.S.C. App. § 1989 (1988).

49 Immigration and Nationality Act of 1952, Pub. L. No. 82–414, 66 Stat. 163, (June 27, 1952).

50 "Woman Communist Leader is Arrested Or Deportation: Woman Communist Leader Seized in Home here in Deportation Case." *New York Times (1923-Current file)*, Jan 21, 1948, pp. 1. *ProQuest*, proxygwa.wrlc.org/login?url=https://search-proquest-com.proxygwa.wrlc.org/docview/108140813?accountid=33473.

51 Carole, Boyce D. "Deportable Subjects: U.S. Immigration Laws and the Criminalizing of Communism." *The South Atlantic Quarterly*, vol. 100, no. 4, 2001, pp. 949–949+. ProQuest, proxygwa.wrlc.org/login?url=https://search-proquest-com.proxygwa.wrlc.org/docview/197293295?accountid=33473.

52 "CLAUDIA JONES LOSES: COMMUNIST FACING OUSTER IS DENIED STAY TO AID CHARNEY." *New York Times (1923-Current file)*, Nov 10, 1955, pp. 39. *ProQuest*, proxygwa.wrlc.org/login?url=https://search-proquest-com.proxygwa.wrlc.org/docview/113336875?accountid=33473.

53 "Convicted Red Leaves Country." *The Atlanta Constitution (1946–1984)*, Dec 10, 1955, pp. 2. ProQuest, proxygwa.wrlc.org/login?url=https://search-proquest-com.proxygwa.wrlc.org/docview/1557769729?accountid=33473.

54 Lynn, Denise. "Socialist Feminism and Triple Oppression: Claudia Jones and African American Women in American Communism."*Journal for the Study of Radicalism*, vol. 8, no. 2, 2014, pp. 1–20.*JSTOR*, www.jstor.org/stable/10.14321/jstudradi.8.2.0001.

55 Sherwood, Marika. *Claudia Jones: A Life in Exile*. London: Lawrence & Wishart, 1999.

56   Puglise, Nicole. "Communist Party Members May Still Be
      Barred from US Citizenship." *The Guardian*, Guardian
      News and Media, 16 Aug. 2016, www.theguardian.com/
      us-news/2016/aug/16/communist-party-members-still-
      barred-us-citizenship-trump.

57   "Filipinos Who Fought for U.S. Sue for Promised
      Citizenship." *Los Angeles Times*, 10 June 1986, www.
      latimes.com/archives/la-xpm-1986-06-10-me-9814-
      story.html.

58   *In re Naturalization of 68 Filipino War Veterans*, 406 F.
      Supp. 931, 936 (1975).

59   Nakano, Satoshi. "NATION, NATIONALISM AND
      CITIZENSHIP IN THE FILIPINO WORLD WAR II
      VETERANS EQUITY MOVEMENT, 1945–1999."
      Hitotsubashi Journal of Social Studies, vol. 32,
      no. 2, 2000, pp. 33–53. JSTOR, www.jstor.org/
      stable/43294595.

60   Immigration and Nationality Act, Pub. L. No. 89–236, 79
      Stat. 911 (1965)

61   *INS vs. Hibi*, 414 U.S. 5 (1973).

62   Ibid.

63   *Quiban v. United States Veterans Admin.,* 713 F.Supp.
      436 (D.D.C.1989); *Quizon v. United States Veterans
      Admin.,* 713 F.Supp. 449 (D.D.C.1989).

64   Immigration Act of 1990, Pub. L. No. 101-649, 104 Stat.
      4978 (1990).

65   https://www.govinfo.gov/content/pkg/CHRG-
      113hhrg89507/html/CHRG-113hhrg89507.htm

66   Guillermo, Emil. "Forgotten: The Battle Thousands of
      WWII Veterans Are Still Fighting." *NBCNews.com*, www.
      nbcnews.com/news/asian-america/forgotten-battle-
      thousands-wwii-veterans-are-still-fighting-n520456.

67   American Reinvestment and Recovery Act, Pub. L. No.
      111-5,§§1002(i), (l), 123 Stat. 115 (2009).

68   Hearing Before the Subcommittee on Oversight and
      Investigations of the Committee of Armed Services.
      "Filipino Veterans Equity Compensation Fund:
      Examining the Department of Defense and Interagency
      Process for Verifying Eligibility." 113th Congress: 2nd
      Session, 24 June 2014, www.govinfo.gov/content/pkg/
      CHRG-113hhrg89507/pdf/CHRG-113hhrg89507.pdf.

69   Eakin, Britain. "World War II Vet Inks Settlement
      on Long-Awaited Benefits." *CNS*, 25 Oct. 2017, www.

courthousenews.com/world-war-ii-vet-inks-settlement-long-awaited-benefits/.

70   Daly, Matthew. "Filipino WWII Veterans Awarded Congressional Gold Medal." *Military Times*, 30 Oct. 2017, www.militarytimes.com/veterans/2017/10/26/filipino-wwii-veterans-awarded-congressional-gold-medal/.

71   Marshall GN, Schell TL, Elliott MN, Berthold SM, Chun C. Mental Health of Cambodian Refugees 2 Decades After Resettlement in the United States. *JAMA*. 2005;294(5):571–579. doi:10.1001/jama.294.5.571

72   "Criminal Justice Reform: What's at Stake for Asian Americans and Pacific Islanders." *Targeted News Service*, Feb 02, 2016. *ProQuest*, proxygwa.wrlc.org/login?url=https://search-proquest-com.proxygwa.wrlc.org/docview/1761975625?accountid=33473.

73   Ibid.

74   Transactional Records Access Clearinghouse. "U.S. Deportation Outcomes by Charge." *TRAC: Immigration*, June 2019, www.trac.syr.edu/phptools/immigration/court_backlog/deport_outcome_charge.php.

75   Raff, Jeremy. "The 'Double Punishment' for Black Undocumented Immigrants." *The Atlantic*, Atlantic Media Company, 3 Jan. 2018, www.theatlantic.com/

politics/archive/2017/12/the-double-punishment-for-black-immigrants/549425/.

76   "Criminal Justice Reform: What's at Stake for Asian Americans and Pacific Islanders." Targeted News Service, Feb 02, 2016. ProQuest

77   Rivas, Jorge. "Another High-Profile Immigrant Rights Activist Has Reportedly Been Detained by ICE." *Splinter*, 8 Mar. 2018, splinternews.com/another-high-profile-immigrant-rights-activist-has-repo-1823593440.

78   Pinto, Nick. "ICE Is Targeting Political Opponents for Deportation, Ravi Ragbir and Rights Groups Say in Court." *The Intercept*, 9 Feb. 2018, theintercept.com/2018/02/09/ravi-ragbir-ice-immigration-deportation.

79   Prendergast, Curt. "Tucson Judge Orders Deportation of Immigrant-, Reproductive-Rights Activist." *Azcentral*, 13 Dec. 2018, www.azcentral.com/story/news/politics/immigration/2018/12/12/tucson-arizona-judge-orders-deportation-activist-alejandra-pablos/2296179002.

80   Shapiro, Nina. "Activist Maru Mora-Villalpando Says ICE Using Deportation Threat as 'Intimidation Tactic'." *The Seattle Times*, 16 Jan. 2018, www.seattletimes.com/seattle-news/activist-maru-mora-villalpando-says-ice-using-her-deportation-as-intimidation-tactic.

81   Burnett, John. "See The 20 Immigration Activists
      Arrested Under Trump." *NPR*, 16 Mar. 2018, www.npr.
      org/2018/03/16/591879718/see-the-20-immigration-
      activists-arrested-under-trump.

83   "MAD WORDS OF WOMAN SET BRAIN IN FLAMES:
      ASSASSIN CZOLGOSZ ASSERTS THAT EMMA
      GOLDMAN INSPIRED HIM WITH A MURDEROUS
      DESIRE." *The Atlanta Constitution* (1881–1945),
      Sep 08, 1901, pp. 2. *ProQuest*, proxygwa.wrlc.org/
      login?url=https://search-proquest-com.proxygwa.wrlc.
      org/docview/495684709?accountid=33473.

84   Immigration Act of March 3, 1903, ch. 1012, 2, 32 Stat.
      1213, 1214, repealed by Immigration Act of February 5,
      1917, ch. 29, 38, 39 Stat. 874, 897. The Immigration Act of
      February 20, 1907, for the most part carried forward the
      ideological exclusions of the 1903 law. See Immigration
      Act of February 20, 1907, ch. 1138, 43, 34 Stat. 898, 899,
      repealed by Immigration Act of February 5, 1917, ch. 29,
      38, 39 Stat. 874, 897.

85   Kraut, Julia Rose. "Global Anti-Anarchism: The Origins
      of Ideological Deportation and the Suppression of
      Expression." *Indiana Journal of Global Legal Studies*,
      vol. 19, no. 1, 2012, pp. 169–193. JSTOR, www.jstor.org/
      stable/10.2979/indjglolegstu.19.1.169.

86   Goldman, Emma (1970). *Living My Life Vol. 1.* Courier Dover Publications. p. 346. ISBN 0-486-22543-7.

87   "ANARCHISTS ARE RAIDED: MURRAY HILL LYCEUM MEETING GOES WILD WITH RAGE. JOHN TURNER TAKEN OFF STAGE LOCKED UP AT ELLIS ISLAND ON WARRANT FROM WASHINGTON, WHICH CHARGES INCITING TO ANARCHY." *New York Times (1857– 1922),* Oct 24, 1903, pp. 1. *ProQuest,* proxygwa.wrlc.org/ login?url=https://search-proquest-com.proxygwa.wrlc. org/docview/96379339?accountid=33473.

88   Graham, Robert. "Emma Goldman: The American Years."*Labour*, no. 58, 2006, pp. 217–225,7. *ProQuest,* proxygwa.wrlc.org/login?url=https:// search-proquest-com.proxygwa.wrlc.org/ docview/218801967?accountid=33473.

89   *Turner v. Williams*, 194 U.S. 279, 293–95(1904) (contemplating meaning of "anarchist" and concluding that Act's exclusion of anarchists was constitutional).

90   Federal Defendants' Memorandum in Opposition to Plaintiffs' Motion for Temporary Restraining Order and Preliminary Injunction, *Pineda-Cruz v. Thompso*n, No. SA-15-CV-326-XR (W.D. Tex. May 7, 2015), 2015 WL 3922298.

91   *Pineda-Cruz v. Thompson*, No. SA-15-CV-326-XR (W.D.
      Tex. Apr. 23, 2015), 2015 WL 1868560.

92   Federal Defendants' Memorandum in Opposition to
      Plaintiffs' Motion for Temporary Restraining Order
      and Preliminary Injunction, *Pineda-Cruz v. Thompson*,
      No. SA-15-CV-326-XR (W.D. Tex. May 7, 2015), 2015
      WL 3922298.

93   Kobach Briefing on NSEERS, 8 Bender's Immigration
      Bull. 277 (Feb. 1, 2003) (discussing National Security
      Entry-Exit Registration System and how it monitors
      persons deemed to be national security concerns).

94   Yee, Lawrence. "Donald Trump Says He Told Us So in
      Anti-Immigrant Orlando Response." *The Wrap*, 12 Jun.
      2016, www.thewrap.com/orlando-massacre-donald-
      trump-tweet-radical-islamic-terrorism/

95   Gilsinan, Kathy. 'Trump Keeps Invoking Terrorism to
      Get His Border Wall." *The Atlantic*, 11 Dec. 2018, www.
      theatlantic.com/international/archive/2018/12/trump-
      incorrectly-links-immigration-terrorism/576358/

96   Harlan Grant Cohen, "Note: The (Un) Favorable
      Judgment of History: Deportation Hearings, the Palmer
      Raids, and the Meaning of History," 78 N.Y.U. L. Rev.
      1431 (2003).

97   "Deportation of Emma Goldman as a Radical 'Alien.' "
      Jewish Women's Archive, jwa.org/thisweek/dec/21/1919/
      emma-goldman.

98   "EMMA GOLDMAN INDICTED.: THREE TRUE
      BILLS FOUND AGAINST HER FOR SPEECHES
      INCITING TO RIOT." *New York Times(1857–1922)*,
      Sep 07, 1893, pp. 4. *ProQuest*, proxygwa.wrlc.org/
      login?url=https://search-proquest-com.proxygwa.wrlc.
      org/docview/95075670?accountid=33473.

99   "EMMA GOLDMAN UNDER ARREST: NEW
      YORK POLICE TAKE THE NOTORIOUS FEMALE
      ANARCHIST, ALEXANDER BERKMAN ALSO
      ARRESTED WITH THE WOMAN." *The Atlanta
      Constitution (1881–1945)*, Jan 07, 1907, pp. 1.
      ProQuest, proxygwa.wrlc.org/login?url=https://
      search-proquest-com.proxygwa.wrlc.org/
      docview/496114803?accountid=33473.

100   "EMMA GOLDMAN AND A. BERKMAN BEHIND
      THE BARS: ANARCHIST HEADQUARTERS
      RAIDED AND LEADERS HELD FOR ANTI-DRAFT
      CONSPIRACY." *New York Times (1857–1922)*,
      Jun 16, 1917, pp. 1. *ProQuest*, proxygwa.wrlc.org/
      login?url=https://search-proquest-com.proxygwa.wrlc.
      org/docview/98160712?accountid=33473.

101 Wireless to THE NEW YORK TIMES. "EXILED
BERKMAN COMMITS SUICIDE: ANARCHIST
AGITATOR, WHO SHOT FRICK IN 1892, DIES
OF BULLET WOUND IN FRANCE." *New York
Times (1923-Current file)*, Jul 02, 1936, pp. 5.
ProQuest, proxygwa.wrlc.org/login?url=https://
search-proquest-com.proxygwa.wrlc.org/
docview/101865799?accountid=33473.

102 Anarchist Act of October 16, 1918, ch. 186, 40 Stat. 1012,
amended by 8 U.S.C. 137 (1925–26) (repealed 1952).

103 Drinnon, Richard. *Rebel in Paradise: A Biography
of Emma Goldman*. Chicago: University of Chicago
Press, 1961.

104 Ibid.

105 "EMMA GOLDMAN FORMALLY WAIVES RIGHT
OF APPEAL." *The Atlanta Constitution (1881–1945)*,
Dec 18, 1919, pp. 1-a4. *ProQuest*, proxygwa.wrlc.org/
login?url=https://search-proquest-com.proxygwa.wrlc.
org/docview/497218004?accountid=33473.

106 Special to THE NEW,YORK TIMES. "ENTRY
PERMITTED TO EMMA GOLDMAN: ANARCHIST
DEPORTED IN 1919 WINS AUTHORITY FOR
90-DAY VISIT WITH RELATIVES." *New York
Times (1923-Current file)*, Jan 10, 1934, pp. 23.

ProQuest, proxygwa.wrlc.org/login?url=https://
search-proquest-com.proxygwa.wrlc.org/
docview/100931239?accountid=33473.

107   Ibid.

108   "EMMA GOLDMAN TO TALK FREELY: DENIES SHE
PROMISED TO IGNORE POLITICS IN LECTURES
ON 'LITERATURE' HERE. ALWAYS BAD, WORSE
NOW' ANARCHIST ON FIRST VISIT SINCE
DEPORTATION IN 1919 SAYS HER IDEAS HAVE
NOT CHANGED." *New York Times (1923-Current file)*,
Feb 03, 1934, pp. 15. *ProQuest*, proxygwa.wrlc.org/
login?url=https://search-proquest-com.proxygwa.wrlc.
org/docview/101085598?accountid=33473.

109   U.S. Dep't of Justice, Immigration and Naturalization
Serv., 1994 Statistical Yearbook of the Immigration
and Naturalization Service 166 (1996) (Table 66: Aliens
Deported by Cause Fiscal Years 1908–80).

110   Lemann, Nicholas. *The Promised Land: The Great Black
Migration and How It Changed America*. New York:
Vintage Books, 1992.

111   Wilkerson, Isabel. *The Warmth of Other Suns*. New York:
Random House, 2010.

112   Hansford, Justin. Jailing a Rainbow: The Marcus Garvey Case, 2016.

113   Ibid.

114   Ibid.

115   Ibid.

116   Ibid.

117   Stein, Judith. The World of Marcus Garvey: Race and Class in Modern Society. New York: ACLS History E-Book Project, 2005.

118   Hansford, Justin. Jailing a Rainbow: The Marcus Garvey Case, 2016.

119   Ibid.

120   Ibid.

121   "GARVEY DENOUNCED AT NEGRO MEETING: POLICE QUIET AUDIENCE AS SPEAKERS ASSAIL "PROVISIONALPRESIDENT OF AFRICA." *New York Times (1857–1922)*, Aug 07, 1922, pp. 7. *ProQuest*, proxygwa.wrlc.org/login?url=https:// search-proquest-com.proxygwa.wrlc.org/ docview/99460994?accountid=33473.

122   Hansford, Justin. Jailing a Rainbow: The Marcus Garvey
       Case, 2016.

123   Taylor, Quintard. From Timbuktu to Katrina: Readings
       in African American History. Australia: Thomson/
       Wadsworth, 2008.

124   "GARVEY SENTENCED TO 5 YEARS IN JAIL:
       BLACK STAR PROMOTER ALSO FINED $1,000
       FOR FRAUDULENT USE OF THE MAILS. GETS
       STAY OF EXECUTION CALLS AMERICA NEGRO'S
       GREATEST FRIEND—PROTEST OUTBREAKS FALL
       TO MATERIALIZE." *New York Times (1923-Current
       file),* Jun 22, 1923, pp. 19. *ProQuest,* proxygwa.wrlc.org/
       login?url=https://search-proquest-com.proxygwa.wrlc.
       org/docview/103198583?accountid=33473.

125   Hansford, Justin, *NOTE: Jailing a Rainbow: The Marcus
       Garvey Case,* 1 Geo. J. L. & Mod. Crit. Race Persp.
       325, 2009.

126   Ibid.

127   Garvey, Amy Jacques. *Garvey and Garveyism.* New York:
       Collier Books, 1970.

128   Vourvoulias, Sabrina, "The Dream Unravels." *AL DÍA
       News,* 13 Nov. 2016, aldianews.com/articles/opinion/
       dream-unravels/32612.

129 Leopold, David, "The DREAM 9's Misguided Protest." *Fox News*, 9 Aug. 2013, www.foxnews.com/opinion/david-leopold-the-dream-9s-misguided-protest.

130 Act of May 19, 1921, Pub. L. No. 67-5, § § 2(a)(6), 3, 42 Stat. 5, 5-6.

131 Immigration Act of 1924, Pub. L. No. 68-139, § 11(a), 43 Stat. 153, 159.

132 "Who Was Shut Out?: Immigration Quotas, 1925–1927." *HISTORY MATTERS—The U.S. Survey Course on the Web*, historymatters.gmu.edu/d/5078.

133 Gibbons, Chip, "The Trial(s) of Harry Bridges." *Jacobin*, 15 Sept. 2016, www.jacobinmag.com/2016/09/harry-bridges-longshore-strike-deportation-communist-party.

134 Irons, Peter, *Politics and Principle: An Assessment of the Roosevelt Record on Civil Rights and Liberties*,59 Wash. L. Rev. 693, 711–16 (1984).

135 U.S. Dep't of Labor, In the Matter of Harry R. Bridges, Findings and Conclusions of the Trial Examiner 132–34 (1939) (on file with the St. Mary's Law Journal) (finding that opposition to "red-baiting" was not equivalent to proof of membership in Communist Party).

136 *Kessler v. Strecker*, 307 U.S. 22 (1939).

137 Gibbons, Chip, "The Trial(s) of Harry Bridges." *Jacobin*, 15 Sept. 2016, www.jacobinmag.com/2016/09/harry-bridges-longshore-strike-deportation-communist-party.

138 Select Committee on Immigration and Refugee Policy, Staff Rep.: U.S. Immigration Policy and the National Interest 737 (1981) (stating that Congress enacted Alien Registration Act in response to Supreme Court's decision in Kessler v. Strecker).

139 *Bridges v. Wixon*, 326 U.S. 135, 140–41 (1945).

140 Ibid.

141 "Trials of Harry Bridges." *New York Times (1923-Current file)*, Apr 09, 1950, pp. 1. *ProQuest*, proxygwa.wrlc.org/login?url=https://search-proquest-com.proxygwa.wrlc.org/docview/111454047?accountid=33473.

142 *United States v. Bridges*, 87 F. Supp. 14 (N.D. Cal. 1949).

143 Ibid.

144 *Bridges v. United States*, 199 F.2d 811, 815 (9th Cir. 1952),*rev'd and remanded,*346 U.S. 209 (1953).

145 Saxon, Wolfgang. "Harry Bridges, Docks Leader, Dies at 88." *The New York Times*, 31 Mar. 1990, www.nytimes.com/1990/03/31/obituaries/harry-bridges-docks-leader-dies-at-88.html.

146   Immigration & Naturalization Service, 1957 Statistical
       Yearbook of the Immigration and Naturalization Service,
       U.S. Department of Justice, stacks.stanford.edu/file/
       dj043hc6989/AnnRepINS1957.pdf

147   Internal Security Act of 1950, 81 P.L. 831, 64 Stat.
       987, 81 Cong. Ch. 1024, 81 P.L. 831, 64 Stat. 987, 81
       Cong. Ch. 1024.

148   Furman, Bess. "360 Citizens Ask Voiding of Internal
       Security Act." *New York Times (1923-Current file),*
       Sep 16, 1955, pp. 1. *ProQuest,* proxygwa.wrlc.org/
       login?url=https://search-proquest-com.proxygwa.wrlc.
       org/docview/113231910?accountid=33473.

149   Hoffman, Abraham. *Unwanted Mexican Americans in
       the Great Depression: Repatriation Pressures, 1929–
       1939.* Tucson: University of Arizona Press, 1979.

150   Garcilazo, Jeffrey M. "McCarthyism, Mexican Americans,
       and the Los Angeles Committee for Protection of the
       Foreign-Born, 1950–1954." *The Western Historical
       Quarterly,* vol. 32, no. 3, 2001, pp. 273–295. JSTOR,
       www.jstor.org/stable/3650736.

151   Ibid.

152   Ibid.

153   Ibid.

154   Ibid.

155   Battisti, Danielle. "The American Committee on Italian
       Migration, Anti-Communism, and Immigration Reform."
       Journal of American Ethnic History, vol. 31, no. 2, 2012,
       pp. 11–40.

156   Morgan, Patricia. *Shame of a Nation: a Documented
       Story of Police-State Terror against Mexican Americans*.
       Los Angeles Committee for Protection of Foreign
       Born, 1954.

157   Arellano, Gustavo. "Whatever Happened to the Santa Ana
       Four?" *OC Weekly*, 12 Jul. 2007, ocweekly.com/news-
       whatever-happened-to-the-santa-ana-four-6426485/.

158   Ibid.

159   Ibid.

160   Ibid.

161   Arellano, Gustavo. "Whatever Happened to the Santa Ana
       Four?" *OC Weekly*, 12 Jul. 2007, ocweekly.com/news-
       whatever-happened-to-the-santa-ana-four-6426485/.

162   Ibid.

163   Fisher, Jerilyn. "Rose Chernin." *Jewish Women: A
       Comprehensive Historical Encyclopedia*, 27 Feb. 2009.

Jewish Women's Archive, jwa.org/encyclopedia/article/chernin-rose.

164 "Rose Chernin, 93, Prominent Leftist." Obituary, *The New York Times*, 16 Sept. 1995, www.nytimes.com/1995/09/16/obituaries/rose-chernin-93-prominent-leftist.html.

165 Ibid.

166 Chernin, Rose. "Organizing the Unemployed in the Bronx in the 1930s (1949)." *History Is A Weapon*, www.historyisaweapon.com/defcon1/chernin1930sbronx.html.

167 Buff, Rachel. "Communist Immigrant Advocates Whom History Erased." *Jewish Currents*, 20 Dec. 2017, jewishcurrents.org/communist-immigrant-advocates-whom-history-erased/.

168 "Rose Chernin; Prosecuted for Communist Activities." *Los Angeles Times*, 16 Sept. 1995, www.latimes.com/archives/la-xpm-1995-09-16-mn-46411-story.html.

169 United States v. Schneiderman, 106 F. Supp. 906, 940, 1952 U.S. Dist. LEXIS 4107, *70

170 *Yates v. United States*, 354 U.S. 298 (1957).

171 Ibid.

172　INA § 212(a)(3)(A)(ii), 8 U.S.C. § 1182(a)(3)(A)(ii).

173　8 U.S.C. § 1424.

174　*United States ex rel. Knauff v. Shaughnessy,* 338 U.S. 537, 539 (1950).

175　Ibid.

176　Ibid.

177　"Mrs. Knauff Is Called a Spy. Immigration Unit Bars Her." *The New York Times*, 27 Mar. 1951, www.nytimes. com/1951/03/27/archives/mrs-knauff-is-called-a-spy-immigration-unit-bars-her-three-say-war.html.

178　Nofil, Brianna. "Note on Detention Camp." *Topic Magazine*, Jun. 2017, www.topic.com/notes-on-detention-camp.

179　Weisselberg, Charles. "ARTICLE: THE EXCLUSION AND DETENTION OF ALIENS: LESSONS FROM THE LIVES OF ELLEN KNAUFF AND IGNATZ MEZEI. " 143 U. Pa. L. Rev. 933, Apr. 1995.

180　"MRS. KNAUFF GETS DEPORTATION STAY: SUPREME COURT JUSTICE GRANTS AT LAST MINUTE REPRIEVE TO PERMIT NEW PLEA FOR HER MRS. KNAUFF GETS DEPORTATION STAY." New York Times (1923-Current file), May 18, 1950,

pp. 1. ProQuest, proxygwa.wrlc.org/login?url=https://
search-proquest-com.proxygwa.wrlc.org/
docview/111696620?accountid=33473.

181 Ibid.

182 "Mrs. Knauff Is Called a Spy. Immigration Unit Bars
Her." *The New York Times*, 27 Mar. 1951, www.nytimes.
com/1951/03/27/archives/mrs-knauff-is-called-a-spy-
immigration-unit-bars-her-three-say-war.html.

183 *In re Ellen Raphael Knauff,* No. A-6937471 (B.I.A. Aug.
29, 1951).

184 "Mrs. Knauff Walks Out of Hearing on Bid to Obtain U. S.
Citizenship: ' New Evidence' Linking German War Bride
to Reds Offered—Applicant, Admitted in 1951, Tearfully
Denies Allegations." *New York Times (1923-Current
file),* Jul 03, 1953, pp. 6. *ProQuest*, proxygwa.wrlc.org/
login?url=https://search-proquest-com.proxygwa.wrlc.
org/docview/112774914?accountid=33473.

185 *Kleindienst v. Mandel*, 408 U.S. 753 (1972).

186 *Int'l Refugee Assistance Project v. Trump*, 265 F. Supp.
3d 570, 586 (2017).

187 *Trump v. Hawaii*, No. 17-965, 585 U.S. ____ (2018).

188   Kruse, Robert J. II (2009). "Geographies of John and Yoko's 1969 Campaign for Peace: An Intersection of Celebrity, Space, Art, and Activism." In Johansson, Ola; Bell, Thomas L. (eds.).*Sound, Society and the Geography of Popular Music*. Ashgate. pp.15–16.

189   Kenworthy, E.W. "Thousands Mark Day: Thousands in Capital Ask Peace." *New York Times (1923-Current file)*, Oct 16, 1969, pp. 1. *ProQuest*, proxygwa.wrlc.org/login?url=https://search-proquest-com.proxygwa.wrlc.org/docview/118540522?accountid=33473.

190   Hunter, Jennifer. "John Lennon, Richard Nixon and a Notorious Legal Battle." *Thestar.com*, 15 Aug. 2016, www.thestar.com/news/insight/2016/08/15/john-lennon-richard-nixon-and-a-notorious-legal-battle.html.

191   *Lennon v. INS*, 527 F.2d 187, 189 (2d Cir. 1975).

192   Wiener, Jon. "John Lennon and Yoko Ono's Deportation Battle." *Los Angeles Times*, 8 Oct. 2010, www.latimes.com/archives/la-xpm-2010-oct-08-la-oe-wiener-john-lennon-deportation-20101008-story.html.

193   "Uncovering The 'Truth' Behind Lennon's FBI Files." *NPR*, 8 Oct. 2010, www.npr.org/templates/story/story.php?storyId=130401193.

194   *Wiener v. FBI*, 943 F.2d 972, 988 (1991).

195 *Lennon v. INS*, 527 F.2d 187, 189 (2d Cir. 1975).

196 Wadhia, Shobha. "The Role of Prosecutorial Discretion in Immigration Law." *Connecticut Public Interest Law Journal* 243 (2010).

197 Wildes, Leon. "The Nonpriority Program of the Immigration and Naturalization Service Goes Public: The Litigative Use of the Freedom of Information Act." 14 San Diego L. Rev. 42, 52–53 (1976).

198 Memorandum from Doris Meissner, Comm'r, Immigration & Naturalization Serv., to Reg'l Dirs., Dist. Dirs., Chief Patrol Agents, Reg'l & Dist. Counsel 2-6, 12 (Nov. 17, 2000).

199 Memorandum from Michael D. Cronin, Acting Assoc. Comm'r, Office of Programs, U.S. Dep't of Justice, to All Reg'l Dirs. 2 (Dec. 22, 1998); Memorandum from William R. Yates, Assoc. Dir. of Operations, U.S. Citizenship & Immigrations Servs., to Dir., Vt. Serv. Ctr. 1-2 (Oct. 8, 2003).

200 Preston, Julia & Cushman, Jr., John. "Obama to Permit Young Migrants to Remain in U.S.," *N.Y. Times*, 15 Jun. 2012, www.nytimes.com/2012/06/16/ us/us-to-stop-deporting-some-illegal-immigrants.html.

201 Neuborne, Burt & Shapiro, Steven, "The Nylon Curtain: America's National Border and the Free Flow of Ideas." 26 WM. & MARY L. REV. 719, 723 (1985).

202 "U.S. STILL BLACKLISTS 3,000 CANADIANS FOR POLITICS." *The New York Times*, 19 Feb. 1984, www.nytimes.com/1984/02/19/world/us-still-blacklists-3000-canadians-for-politics.html.

203 Akram, Susan. "ARTICLE: SCHEHEREZADE MEETS KAFKA: TWO DOZEN SORDID TALES OF IDEOLOGICAL EXCLUSION." 14 Geo. Immigr. L.J. 51, 94, Fall 1999.

204 Shehadeh, Michel. ""A Never-Ending Saga": The Case of "the Los Angeles Eight."" *The Washington Report on Middle East Affairs*, vol. XV, no. 8, 05, 1997, pp. 33. *ProQuest*, proxygwa.wrlc.org/login?url=https://search-proquest-com.proxygwa.wrlc.org/docview/218783003?accountid=33473.

205 Butterfield, Jeanne A. "Do Immigrants Have First Amendment Rights? Revisiting the Los Angeles Eight Case." *Middle East Report*, no. 212, 1999, pp. 4–6. *JSTOR*, www.jstor.org/stable/3012904.

206 Ibid.

207 Cole, David. "License for a Witch Hunt." *Washington Post*, May 19, 1996, at C9, www.washingtonpost.com/archive/opinions/1996/05/19/license-for-a-witch-hunt/68a7d4b6-7a63-45db-ac12-7e81b55fa789/?utm_term=.8fcf0b2fa444.

208 Akram, Susan. "ARTICLE: SCHEHEREZADE MEETS KAFKA: TWO DOZEN SORDID TALES OF IDEOLOGICAL EXCLUSION." 14 Geo. Immigr. L.J. 51, 94, Fall 1999.

209 IMMIGRATION ACT OF 1990, 1990 Enacted S. 358, 101 Enacted S. 358, 104 Stat. 4978, 101 P.L. 649, 1990 Enacted S. 358, 101 Enacted S. 358.

210 Ibid.

211 8 U.S.C. § 1251(a)(4)(B) (1990).

212 Butterfield, Jeanne A. "Do Immigrants Have First Amendment Rights? Revisiting the Los Angeles Eight Case." *Middle East Report*, no. 212, 1999, pp. 4–6. *JSTOR*, www.jstor.org/stable/3012904.

213 *Reno v. American-Arab Anti-Discrimination Comm.*, 525 U.S. 471 (1999).

214 Ibid.

215 Shehadeh, Michel. "Charges Dropped against Last of 'Los Angeles Eight'." *SFGate*, San Francisco Chronicle, 10 Feb. 2012, www.sfgate.com/opinion/article/Charges-dropped-against-last-of-Los-Angeles-3234293.php.

216 Comprehensive Immigration Reform: The Future of Undocumented Immigrant Students: Hearing Before the Subcomm. on Immigration, Citizenship, Refugees, Border Security, and International Law of the H. Comm. on the Judiciary, 110th Cong. (2007), judiciary.house.gov/hearings/printers/110th/35453.PDF.

217 Ibid.

218 Ibid.

219 Ii, Martin Kady. "Tancredo: Arrest the Immigrant Students at Press Conference." *POLITICO*, 23 Oct. 2007, www.politico.com/blogs/politico-now/2007/10/tancredo-arrest-the-immigrant-students-at-press-conference-003781.

220 Wong, Kent, and Matias Ramos. "Undocumented and Unafraid: Tam Tran and Cinthya Felix." *Boom: A Journal of California*, vol. 1, no. 1, 2011, pp. 10–14. *JSTOR*, www.jstor.org/stable/10.1525/boom.2011.1.1.10.

221 Ibid.

222 Ibid.

223 Ibid.

224 Bell, Alex. "Tam Tran GS Killed in Car Accident." *Brown Daily Herald*, 16 May 2010, www.browndailyherald. com/web-update-tam-tran-gs-killed-in-car-accident-1.2266300.

225 Preston, Julia. "Illegal Immigrant Students Protest at McCain Office." *The New York Times*, 18 May 2010, www. nytimes.com/2010/05/18/us/18dream.html.

226 Hinton, Kip Austin. "Undocumented Citizens: The Civic Engagement of Activist Immigrants." *Education, Citizenship and Social Justice*, vol. 10, no. 2, July 2015, pp. 152–167, doi:10.1177/1746197915583933.

227 García, Sandra E. "U.S. Requiring Social Media Information From Visa Applicants." *The New York Times*, 2 Jun. 2019, www.nytimes.com/2019/06/02/us/us-visa-application-social-media.html.

228 Gates, Gary, J. "LGBT Adult Immigrants in the United States." *The Williams Institute*, March 2013, williamsinstitute.law.ucla.edu/research/census-lgbt-demographics-studies/us-lgbt-immigrants-mar-2013/.

229 Immigration and Nationality Act of 1917, Pub. L. No. 64-301, § 19, 39 Stat. 874, 889 (1917) (codified as amended at 8 U.S.C. § 1227 (2006)).

230 *Whitewood v. Wolf,* 992 F. Supp. 2d 410, 427 (M.D. Pa. 2014) (internal citations omitted).

231 Johnson, David K. *The Lavender Scare: The Cold War Persecution of Gays and Lesbians in the Federal Government.* Chicago: University of Chicago Press, 2004.

232 Ibid.

233 The Immigration and Nationality Act of 1952 excluded "aliens afflicted with a psychopathic personality, epilepsy, or a mental defect." In 1965, Congress eliminated epilepsy and added "sexual deviation." Immigration and Nationality Act of 1952, 212(a)(4), Pub. L. No. 414, 66 Stat. 163, 182, amended by Act of Oct. 3, 1965, Pub. L. No. 89-236, 15(b), 79 Stat. 911, 919 (codified as amended at 8 U.S.C. 1182(a)(4) (1988) (repealed 1990)). The entire provision was eliminated by the Immigration Act of 1990, Pub. L. No. 101-649, 104 Stat. 4978 (1990).

234 Stein, Marc. *Sexual Injustice: Supreme Court Decisions from Griswold to Roe.* Chapel Hill: University of North Carolina Press, 2010.

235 *Rosenberg v. Fleuti,* 374 U.S. 449 (1963).

236 *Fleuti v. Rosenberg,* 302 F.2d 652 (1962).

237 Canaday, Margot. " 'Who Is a Homosexual?": The Consolidation of Sexual Identities in Mid-Twentieth-

Century American Immigration Law." *Law & Social Inquiry*, vol. 28, no. 2, 2003, pp. 351–386. JSTOR, www.jstor.org/stable/1215774.

238　S. Rep. No. 748, 89th Cong., 1st Sess. 19, reprinted in 1965 U.S. Code Cong. & Ad. News 3328, 3337; H.R. Rep. No. 745, 89th Cong., 1st Sess. 16 (1965).

239　Canaday, Margot. " 'Who Is a Homosexual?'": The Consolidation of Sexual Identities in Mid-Twentieth-Century American Immigration Law." *Law & Social Inquiry*, vol. 28, no. 2, 2003, pp. 351–386. JSTOR, www.jstor.org/stable/1215774.

240　Luibheid, Eithne. " 'Looking like a Lesbian': The Organization of Sexual Monitoring at the United States-Mexican Border." *Journal of the History of Sexuality*, vol. 8, no. 3, 1998, pp. 477–506.*JSTOR*, www.jstor.org/stable/3704873.

241　Ibid.

242　8 U.S.C. § 1224.

243　8 U.S.C. § 1226(d).

244　Luibheid, Eithne. " 'Looking like a Lesbian': The Organization of Sexual Monitoring at the United States-Mexican Border." *Journal of the History of Sexuality*, vol. 8, no. 3, 1998, pp. 477–506.*JSTOR*, www.jstor.org/stable/3704873.

245 Ibid.

246 Ibid.

247 *Boutilier v. Immigration & Naturalization Service*, 363 F.2d 488 (1966).

248 Ibid.

249 Stein, Marc. "Boutilier and the U.S. Supreme Court's Sexual Revolution," *Law and History Review* 23 (2005), 491–536.

250 Ibid.

251 *Boutilier v. INS*, 387 U.S. 118, 123 (1967).

252 Stein, Marc. "Boutilier and the U.S. Supreme Court's Sexual Revolution," *Law and History Review* 23 (2005), 491–536.

253 Ibid.

254 By, BOYCE R. "Psychiatrists Review Stand on Homosexuals: Statement to be Drafted Term Misused'." *New York Times (1923-Current file)*, Feb 09, 1973, pp. 24. *ProQuest*, proxygwa.wrlc.org/login?url=https://

search-proquest-com.proxygwa.wrlc.org/
docview/119695648?accountid=33473.

255 American Psychiatric Association, Diagnostic and
Statistical Manual of Mental Disorders (2d ed. 1967)
(rev. 1974).

256 Bushell, Logan. "Give Me Your Tired, Your Poor,
Your Huddled Masses"—Just as Long as They Fit
the Heteronormative Ideal: U.S. Immigration Law's
Exclusionary & Inequitable Treatment of Lesbian, Gay,
Bisexual, Transgendered, and Queer Migrants." *Gonzaga
Law Review*, 48: 674–700, 2013.

257 *Adams v. Howerton*, 486 F. Supp. 1119, 1121 (C.D.
Cal. 1980).

258 *Adams*, 486 F. Supp. at 1125.

259 *Adams v. Howerton*, 673 F.2d 1036 (9th Cir.), *cert.
denied*, 458 U.S. 1111, 73 L. Ed. 2d 1373, 102 S. Ct.
3494 (1982).

260 *Sullivan v. Immigration & Naturalization Service*, 772
F.2d 609, 611 (1985).

261 Masters, Troy. "United States Government Says L.A.
Gay Couple's 1975 Marriage Is Valid." *The Pride LA*,
7 June 2017, thepridela.com/2016/06/united-states-
government-says-gay-couples-1975-marriage-is-valid/.

262 Franco, Daniela. "For Four Decades, This Same-Sex Couple Fought to Marry." *TakePart*, 15 June 2015, www.takepart.com/article/2015/06/15/four-decades-same-sex-couple-fought-marry.

263 *United States v. Windsor*, 570 U.S. 744 (2013).

264 Margolin, Emma. "Gay Widower Renews Call for Marriage-Based Green Card." *MSNBC*, NBCUniversal News Group, 21 Apr. 2014, www.msnbc.com/msnbc/anthony-sullivan-the-gay-rights-pioneer-you-havent-heard.

265 Phillips, Craig. "US Recognizes Marriage of Tony Sullivan and Richard Adams." *PBS*, 8 June 2016, www.pbs.org/independentlens/blog/united-states-officially-recognizes-tony-sullivan-richard-adamss-marriage/.

266 Fitzgerald, Michael. "U.S. Government Finally Recognizes Groundbreaking Gay Couple's 1975 Marriage—VIDEO." *Towleroad Gay News*, 8 June 2016, www.towleroad.com/2016/06/u-s-government-finally-recognizes-groundbreaking-gay-couples-1975-marriage-video/.

267 JOSEPH B. "Homosexuals Still Fight U.S. Immigration Limits: 'Health Service View." *New York Times (1923-Current file)*, Aug 12, 1979, pp. 20. *ProQuest*, proxygwa.wrlc.org/login?url=https://

search-proquest-com.proxygwa.wrlc.org/
docview/120737969?accountid=33473.

268 *Lesbian/Gay Freedom Day Committee, Inc. v. United
     States Immigration & Naturalization Service,* 541 F.
     Supp. 569 (1982).

269 Memorandum from Julius Richmond, Assistant Secretary
     for Health, United States Department of Health,
     Education and Welfare, and Surgeon General, to William
     Foege and George Lythcott (August 2, 1979).

270 Special to The New York Times. "U.S. Drops Rule Barring
     Suspected Homosexuals: Outlook Not Clear Directive
     Held a Victory." *New York Times (1923-Current file),*
     Aug 15, 1979, pp. 1. *ProQuest,* proxygwa.wrlc.org/
     login?url=https://search-proquest-com.proxygwa.wrlc.
     org/docview/120762148?accountid=33473.

271 Pear, Robert. "Ban is Affirmed on Homosexuals
     Entering Nation: Justice Dept. Office Rules Law must
     be Enforced no Count on those Excluded Temporary
     Order Issued." *New York Times (1923-Current file),*
     Dec 27, 1979, pp. 1. *ProQuest,* proxygwa.wrlc.org/
     login?url=https://search-proquest-com.proxygwa.wrlc.
     org/docview/123869024?accountid=33473.

272 Ibid.

273 Guilfoy, Chris. "Immigration Board Hears Arguments in Hill Case." *Gay Community News*, vol. 8, no. 34, Mar 21, 1981, pp. 3. *ProQuest*, proxygwa.wrlc.org/login?url=https://search-proquest-com.proxygwa.wrlc.org/docview/199332503?accountid=33473.

274 Ibid.

275 *Lesbian/Gay Freedom Day Committee, Inc. v. United States Immigration & Naturalization Service,* 541 F. Supp. 569, 574 (1982).

276 Ibid.

277 Shehadi, Philip. "'we did this on Purpose' Dutch Gays Come to NY, Protest Immigration Laws." *Gay Community News*, vol. 8, no. 37, Apr 11, 1981, pp. 1. *ProQuest*, proxygwa.wrlc.org/login?url=https://search-proquest-com.proxygwa.wrlc.org/docview/199320491?accountid=33473.

278 Daniel, Dan. "Bear Capron can't Come Home." *Gay Community News*, vol. 7, no. 30, Feb 23, 1980, pp. 3. *ProQuest*, proxygwa.wrlc.org/login?url=https://search-proquest-com.proxygwa.wrlc.org/docview/199393622?accountid=33473.

279 Ibid.

280 France, David. "Injunction Bans Anti-Gay Policy in
     Immigration." *Gay Community News*, vol. 10, no.
     3, Jul 31, 1982, pp. 1. *ProQuest*, proxygwa.wrlc.org/
     login?url=https://search-proquest-com.proxygwa.wrlc.
     org/docview/199313718?accountid=33473.

281 *Hill v. United States Immigration & Naturalization
     Service*, 714 F.2d 1470, 1480 (1983).

282 *Matter of Longstaff*, 716 F.2d 1439, 1441 (5th Cir. 1983)

283 Clark, Jill. "Gay/Lesbian Immigration Threatened by
     Reform Bill." *Gay Community News*, vol. 10, no. 47,
     Jun 18, 1983, pp. 1. *ProQuest*, proxygwa.wrlc.org/
     login?url=https://search-proquest-com.proxygwa.wrlc.
     org/docview/199383452?accountid=33473.

284 Immigration Act of 1990, Pub. L. No. 101-649, 104 Stat.
     4978 (1990).

285 Rodrigues, Jason. "50 Years of Castro: Timeline of
     Fidel Castro's Rule in Cuba." *The Guardian*, Guardian
     News and Media, 1 Jan. 2009, www.theguardian.com/
     world/2009/jan/01/fidel-castro-raul-cuba.

286 Larzelere, Alex. *Castro's Ploy—America's Dilemma: The
     1980 Cuban Boatlift*. Washington: National Defense
     University Press, 1988.

287 "20,000 Gays Reported in Boatlift." *The Atlanta Constitution (1946–1984),* Jul 07, 1980, pp. 1. *ProQuest,* proxygwa.wrlc.org/login?url=https://search-proquest-com.proxygwa.wrlc.org/docview/1630115329?accountid=33473.

288 Peña, Susana. " 'Obvious Gays' and the State Gaze: Cuban Gay Visibility and U.S. Immigration Policy during the 1980 Mariel Boatlift." *Journal of the History of Sexuality,* vol. 16, no. 3, 2007, pp. 482–514. *JSTOR,* www.jstor.org/stable/30114194.

289 Montgomery, Paul L. "Year Later, 1,800 Cubans Wait in U.S. Jails: One Year Later, 1,800 Cubans Remain in U.S. Jails Applied for Emigration Problems at Fort Chaffee Forced to Cut Sugar Cane 'in a Cage Like an Animal'." *New York Times (1923-Current file),* Apr 27, 1981, pp. 1. *ProQuest,* proxygwa.wrlc.org/login?url=https://search-proquest-com.proxygwa.wrlc.org/docview/121849226?accountid=33473.

290 Wilkinson, Tracy. "Cubans Wait without Hope: For Refugees, U.S. Camps are Concentration of Pain and Fear." *The Atlanta Constitution (1946–1984),* Sep 07, 1980, pp. 2. *ProQuest,* proxygwa.wrlc.org/login?url=https://search-proquest-com.proxygwa.wrlc.org/docview/1614193212?accountid=33473.

291 Morris, David. "Gay Cuban Refugees here: Where do Feds Send them?" *Gay Community News*, vol. 7, no. 47, Jun 21, 1980, pp. 1. *ProQuest*, proxygwa.wrlc.org/login?url=https://search-proquest-com.proxygwa.wrlc.org/docview/199296547?accountid=33473.

292 Paul, Heath H. "FORT CHAFFEE'S UNWANTED CUBANS: CUBANS." *New York Times (1923-Current file)*, Dec 21, 1980, pp. 5. *ProQuest*, proxygwa.wrlc.org/login?url=https://search-proquest-com.proxygwa.wrlc.org/docview/121418539?accountid=33473.

293 Crewdson, John M. "Hundreds in Boats, Defying U.S., Sail for Cuba to Pick Up Refugees: Hundreds in Boats, Defying Authorities, Sail to Cuba to Rescue Kin Refugees Let in 'Conditionally'." *New York Times (1923-Current file)*, Apr 25, 1980, pp. 2. *ProQuest*, proxygwa.wrlc.org/login?url=https://search-proquest-com.proxygwa.wrlc.org/docview/121177925?accountid=33473.

294 Refugee Act of 1980. Pub. L. 96-212. 94 Stat. 102. 17 March 1980.

295 Capó Jr., Julio. "Queering Mariel: Mediating Cold War Foreign Policy and U.S. Citizenship among Cuba's Homosexual Exile Community, 1978–1994." *Journal of American Ethnic History*, vol. 29, no. 4, 2010,

pp. 78–106. *JSTOR*, www.jstor.org/stable/10.5406/
jamerethnhist.29.4.0078.

296 Dewitt, Karen. "HOMOSEXUAL CUBANS GET
SETTLEMENT AID: TWO U.S. ORGANIZATIONS
ASSIST IN SEEKING SPONSORS FOR SOME AMONG
FT. CHAFFEE EXILES SOME GETTING PRIORITY
'STILL HIDING OUR FEATHERS' DECLARATION TO
AID ESCAPE." *New York Times (1923-Current file)*,
Aug 17, 1980, pp. 34. *ProQuest*, proxygwa.wrlc.org/
login?url=https://search-proquest-com.proxygwa.wrlc.
org/docview/121048789?accountid=33473.

297 Ibid.

298 Stuart, Reginald. "3 Years Later, most Cubans of
Boatlift Adjusting to U.S.: After 3 Years, most Cubans
Adjusting." *New York Times (1923-Current file)*,
May 17, 1983, pp. 2. *ProQuest*, proxygwa.wrlc.org/
login?url=https://search-proquest-com.proxygwa.wrlc.
org/docview/122288902?accountid=33473.

299 Crewdson, John. "CUBA LINK SOUGHT IN SPREAD
OF AIDS." *Chicagotribune.com*, 3 Sept. 2018, www.
chicagotribune.com/news/ct-xpm-1988-01-31-
8803260544-story.html.

300 Immigration Act of 1891, 26 Stat. 1084 (1891).

301 Supplemental Appropriations Act of 1987, Pub. L. No. 100-71, § 518, 101 Stat. 475 (1987).

302 Immigration Act of 1990, Pub. L. No. 101-649, 104 Stat. 4978 (1990).

303 Morrow, Rona. "AIDS and Immigration: The United States Attempts to Deport a Disease." *The University of Miami Inter-American Law Review*, vol. 20, no. 1, 1988, pp. 131–173. *JSTOR*, www.jstor.org/stable/40176173.

304 Pendleton, Faith G. "The United States Exclusion of HIV-Positive Aliens: Realities and Illusions." *Suffolk Transnational Law Review* 18 (1995).

305 Ratner, Michael. "How We Closed the Guantanamo HIV Camp: The Intersection of Politics and Litigation." *Harvard Human Rights Journal* 11 (Spring 1998): 187–220.

306 *Haitian Centers Council, Inc. v. Sale*, 823 F. Supp. 1028 (E.D.N.Y. 1993), *vacated by* Stipulated Order Approving Class Action Settlement (Feb. 22, 1994), *abrogation recognized by Cuban American Bar Assoc., Inc. v. Christopher*, 43 F.3d 1412, 1424 n.8 (11th Cir. 1995).

307 National Institutes of Health Revitalization Act of 1993, Pub. L. 103-43, 107 Stat. 122 (1993).

308 National Defense Authorization Act for Fiscal Year
     1994, Pub. L. No. 103-160, 572, 107 Stat. 160, 1670-73
     (codified as amended at 10 U.S.C. 654 (2000)); Dep't
     of Def., Directive No. 1332.14, Enlisted Administrative
     Separations (1993) (effective Feb. 5, 1994).

309 Defense of Marriage Act of 1996 § 7, 1 U.S.C. § 7 (2006); 8
     U.S.C. § 1154(a)-(b) (2006).

310 9 U.S. DEP'T OF STATE, FOREIGN AFFAIRS MANUAL §
     40.11 N.9.1-2 (June 5, 2012), www.state.gov/documents/
     organization/86936.pdf.

311 Uniting American Families Act, H.R. 1024, 111th Cong.
     (2009); Uniting American Families Act, S. 424, 111th
     Cong. (2009); Uniting American Families Act, H.R. 2221,
     110th Cong. (2007); Uniting American Families Act, S.
     1328, 110th Cong. (2007).

312 *United States v. Windsor*, 570 U.S. 744 (2013).

313 Hansler, Jennifer, and Richard Roth. "US Halting Visas
     for Same-Sex Partners of Diplomats." *CNN*, 2 Oct. 2018,
     www.cnn.com/2018/10/02/politics/same-sex-couples-
     diplomatic-visas/index.html.

314 147 Cong. Rec. S8,581 (daily ed. Aug. 1, 2001) (statement
     of Sen. Orrin Hatch).

315 Olivio, Antonio. "Immigration Battle Has 2 Fronts for Gays, Lesbians." *Chicago Tribune*, 25 Dec. 2007, www.chicagotribune.com/news/ct-xpm-2007-12-25-0712240777-story.html

316 Olivio, Antonio. "Youth step up in immigration debate; Student group working to push reform effort through." *Chicago Tribune*, 18 Jan. 2010, www.chicagotribune.com/news/ct-xpm-2010-01-18-1001170165-story.html

317 Hing, Julianne. "In the Age of Trump, Tania Unzueta Is Holding Democrats to Account." *The Nation*, 11 Jan. 2018, www.thenation.com/article/tania-unzueta-on-holding-democrats-to-account-in-the-age-of-trump/.

318 "Chicago Woman Sues Homeland Security After DACA Renewal Denied." *CBS Chicago,* 25 May 2016, chicago.cbslocal.com/2016/05/25/woman-sues-after-daca-denied/.

319 "USCIS Reverses Decision to Punish Civil Disobedience, Grants DACA to Chicago Youth." *National Immigrant Justice Center*, www.immigrantjustice.org/node/13046.

320 Jobin-Leeds, Greg et. al. *When We Fight, We Win: Twenty-first-century Social Movements and the Activists That Are Transforming Our World.* The New Press, 2016.

321 Asian Law Caucus et al. "Education Not Deportation: A Guide for Undocumented Youth in Removal Proceedings." *Advancing Justice—Asian Law Caucus* 2012, www.advancingjustice-alc.org/wp-content/uploads/2012/11/Education-Not-Deportation-A-Guide-for-Undocumented-Youth-in-Removal-Proceedings-2.pdf.

322 Corrunker, Laura. " 'Coming Out of the Shadows': DREAM Act Activism in the Context of Global Anti-Deportation Activism." *Indiana Journal of Global Legal Studies*, vol. 19, no. 1, 2012, pp. 143–168. *JSTOR*, www.jstor.org/stable/10.2979/indjglolegstu.19.1.143.

323 "Senate Passes 'Don't Ask, Don't Tell' Repeal; DREAM Act Fails." *CNN*, 18 Dec. 2010, www.cnn.com/2010/POLITICS/12/18/dadt.dream.act/index.html.

324 Zamorano, Neidi Dominguez, et al. "DREAM Activists: Rejecting the Passivity of the Nonprofit, Industrial Complex." *Truthout*, truthout.org/articles/dream-activists-rejecting-the-passivity-of-the-nonprofit-industrial-complex/.

325 Gammage, Jeff. "Gay, Trans Activists Come to Philly from across the U.S., Will Strategize over Treatment by Immigration Enforcement Agencies." *The Philadelphia Inquirer*, 17 May 2019, www.inquirer.com/news/

gay-trans-queer-immigrant-immigration-ice-detention-20190517.html.

326 Vargas, Andrew S. "'Osito' Is an Honest, Edgy Comedy About 'Homo-Hetero' Friendship From Two Undocumented Activists." *Remezcla*, 12 Dec. 2016, remezcla.com/film/osito-crowdfunding-season-4-julio-salgado/.

327 CultureStrike Team. "Writing Their Own Story: Two Undocumented Artists on Their New TV Pilot." *Pop Culture Collaborative*, 19 Mar. 2019, popcollab.org/writing-their-own-story/.

328 Vargas, Jose Antonio. "My Life as an Undocumented Immigrant." *The New York Times*, 22 June 2011, www.nytimes.com/2011/06/26/magazine/my-life-as-an-undocumented-immigrant.html.

329 Vera, Amir. "Undocumented Immigrant Jose Antonio Vargas Gets School Named after Him." *CNN*, 19 June 2018, www.cnn.com/2018/06/18/us/jose-antonio-vargas-school/index.html.

330 Gerace, Miriam, and Ruthie Epstein. "Opinion: The Dream 9, Immigration Detention and Solitary Confinement." *NBC Latino*, 9 Aug. 2013, nbclatino.com/2013/08/09/opinion-the-dream-9-immigration-detention-and-solitary-confinement/.

331 Serrato, Jacqueline. "Queer Chicagoan Who Turned Herself in to Border Patrol Granted Asylum." *Chicago Tribune*, 13 Dec. 2018, www.chicagotribune.com/hoy/ct-queer-chicagoan-who-defied-border-patrol-granted-asylum-20180624-story.html.

332 Rivas, Jorge. "Meet Jennicet, One Month after She Interrupted President Obama." *Splinter*, 24 July 2017, splinternews.com/meet-jennicet-one-month-after-she-interrupted-presiden-1793849645.

333 Gross, Daniel A. "The U.S. Government Turned Away Thousands of Jewish Refugees, Fearing That They Were Nazi Spies." *Smithsonian.com*, Smithsonian Institution, 18 Nov. 2015, www.smithsonianmag.com/history/us-government-turned-away-thousands-jewish-refugees-fearing-they-were-nazi-spies-180957324/.

334 "Deja Vu for Rights Lawyer: Peter Schey Is Jumping Into the Fight Against Prop. 187—Much Like the Battle He Helped Win for Texas Students." *Los Angeles Times*, Los Angeles Times, 10 Nov. 1994, www.latimes.com/archives/la-xpm-1994-11-10-ls-61008-story.html.

335 *Plyler v. Doe*, 457 U.S. 202 (1982).

336 "Major Portions of Prop. 187 Thrown Out by Federal Judge: Immigration: U.S. Law Preempts State from barring Federally Funded Services to Those in the

Country Illegally, Ruling Says. Issues Are Expected to Be Decided Eventually by Supreme Court." *Los Angeles Times*, 21 Nov. 1995, www.latimes.com/archives/la-xpm-1995-11-21-mn-5597-story.html.

337 "How a 35-Year-Old Case of a Migrant Girl from El Salvador Still Fuels the Border Debate | CBC Radio." *CBC/Radio Canada*, 28 June 2019, www.cbc.ca/radio/day6/detained-migrant-children-resident-orcas-stranger-things-stonewall-at-50-and-more-1.5192640/how-a-35-year-old-case-of-a-migrant-girl-from-el-salvador-still-fuels-the-border-debate-1.5192662.

338 *Reno v. Flores*, 507 U.S. 292 (1993).

339 Obser, Katharina. "Why Is the Administration Doubling down on Family Detention?" *TheHill*, 4 Feb. 2016, thehill.com/blogs/congress-blog/civil-rights/227717-why-is-the-administration-doubling-down-on-family-detention.

340 Sargent, Greg. "Hillary: Minors Crossing Border Must Be Sent Home." *The Washington Post*, WP Company, 18 June 2014, www.washingtonpost.com/blogs/plum-line/wp/2014/06/18/hillary-minors-crossing-border-must-be-sent-home/?utm_term=.d2143a074da0.

341 Robinson, Eugene. "The Trump Administration Kidnapped Children. Someone Should Go to Jail." *The Washington Post*, WP Company, 12 July 2018,

www.washingtonpost.com/opinions/the-trump-administration-kidnapped-children-someone-should-go-to-jail/2018/07/12/2128c51c-8605-11e8-8f6c-46cb43e3f306_story.html.

342 Bogado, Aura, and Patrick Michels. "US Government Uses Several Clandestine Shelters to Detain Immigrant Children." *Reveal*, 19 Mar. 2019, www.revealnews.org/article/us-government-uses-several-clandestine-shelters-to-detain-immigrant-children/.

343 Goldsmith, Susan. "L.A. Lawyer Peter Schey Ruining America by Helping Hordes of Illegal Immigrants Stay Here." *New Times L.A.,* 20 Jun. 2002, available online at www.freerepublic.com/focus/news/705251/posts.

344 Carcamo, Cindy, and Esquivel, Paloma. "This Immigrant Rights Champion Runs a Migrant Youth Home That Was Repeatedly Cited for Safety Violations." *Los Angeles Times*, 22 May 2019, www.latimes.com/projects/la-me-immigrant-children-group-home-casa-libre-peter-schey/.

345 Cole, Wendy. "Person of the Year 2006." *Time*, Time Inc., 25 Dec. 2006, content.time.com/time/specials/packages/article/0,28804,2019341_2017328_2017183,00.html.

346 "Southwest Border Migration FY 2019."*Southwest Border Migration FY 2019 | U.S. Customs and Border

Protection, www.cbp.gov/newsroom/stats/sw-border-migration.

347 González, Gilbert G. "Organizations Serving Latino Communities Take Opposing Positions on Senate Bill 744."*Diálogo*, vol. 18 no. 2, 2015, pp. 7–20. Project MUSE, doi:10.1353/dlg.2015.0001

348 Weiner, Rachel. "How Immigration Reform Failed, over and Over." *The Washington Post*, WP Company, 30 Jan. 2013, www.washingtonpost.com/news/the-fix/wp/2013/01/30/how-immigration-reform-failed-over-and-over/?utm_term=.37d56643e43e.

349 Ordoñez, Franco. "Trump Administration Hits Some Immigrants In U.S. Illegally With Fines Up To $500,000." *NPR*, 2 July 2019, www.npr.org/2019/07/02/738059913/trump-administration-sends-out-notices-of-500-000-fines-for-those-in-u-s-illegal.

350 "Infiltrating ICE: How Undocumented Activists Are Organizing on the Inside." *videonation*, Youtube, 7 Feb. 2013, www.youtube.com/watch?v=7uy6S_0-I_M.

351 "DREAMers Infiltrate Immigration Detention Center." *DreamActivistdotorg*, Youtube, 2 Aug. 2012, www.youtube.com/watch?v=QPqEuTop41g.

352   Ibid.

353   Ibid.

354   Niarchos, Stavros. "La Morada." *The New Yorker*, vol. 93,
      no. 30, Oct 02, 2017, pp. 15. *ProQuest*, proxygwa.wrlc.
      org/login?url=https://search-proquest-com.proxygwa.
      wrlc.org/docview/1947003716?accountid=33473.

355   Hing, Julianne. "Alabama DREAMers Speak From
      Detention: ICE Is 'Rogue Agency.' "*Colorlines*, 28 July
      2016, www.colorlines.com/articles/alabama-dreamers-
      speak-detention-ice-rogue-agency.

356   Heredia, Luisa. "Of Radicals and DREAMers:
      Harnessing Exceptionality to Challenge Immigration
      Control." *Association of Mexican-American Educators*,
      Vol. 9, Iss. 3, 2015, pdfs.semanticscholar.org/
      a922/1bade35ca56fad8e23de8652039ad93cf215.pdf

357   "DREAM Activist: I Infiltrated Florida Facility to Expose
      How U.S. Still Detaining Youth Immigrants." *Democracy
      Now!*, Aug. 8, 2012, www.democracynow.org/2012/8/8/
      dream_activist_i_infiltrated_florida_facility

358   Heredia, Luisa L. "More than DREAMs."*NACLA
      Report on the Americas*, vol. 48, no. 1, Spring,
      2016, pp. 59–67. *ProQuest*, proxygwa.wrlc.org/

login?url=https://search-proquest-com.proxygwa.wrlc.
org/docview/1866259515?accountid=33473.

359 O'Matz, Megan. "Immigrants with No Criminal History
Get Lengthy Stays at Little-Known Jail." *Sun*, 10 Oct.
2018, www.sun-sentinel.com/news/fl-xpm-2013-01-05-
fl-private-immigration-jail-20130105-story.html.

360 Clary, Mike. "Detained Immigrant on Day 18 of Hunger
Strike." *Sun*, 10 Oct. 2018, articles.sun-sentinel.
com/2012-08-09/news/fl-detention-center-hunger-
strike-20120808_1_deportation-cases-immigration-and-
customs-enforcement-hunger-strike.

361 Ibid.

362 "The Infiltrators' Film Aims to Open Americans' Eyes to
the Reality of Deportation." *Public Radio International*,
www.pri.org/stories/2019-03-18/infiltrators-film-aims-
open-americans-eyes-reality-deportation.

363 Rojas, Claudio. "Claudio Rojas Shares How He Got
Deported to Argentina (Spanish)." *Miami Herald*, 4 Apr.
2019, www.miamiherald.com/news/local/immigration/
article228862594.html.

364 Lal, Prerna. "NIYA Organizers Infiltrate Michigan ICE
to Reveal Racial Profiling and Due Process Abuses."
Lifted Lamp, 15 Apr. 2013, liftedlamp.wordpress.

com/2013/04/15/niya-organizers-infiltrate-michigan-ice-to-reveal-racial-profiling-and-due-process-abuses/

365 Rivera, Angy. "Dreaming with My Mother." *The Progressive*, vol. 76, no. 11, 11, 2012, pp. 32–33. *ProQuest*, proxygwa.wrlc.org/login?url=https://search-proquest-com.proxygwa.wrlc.org/docview/1115473887?accountid=33473.

366 Goodman, Jillian. "Advice for the Undocumented: Colombian-Born College Student Angy Rivera has Become the Movement's Dear Abby." *New York*, Jul 09, 2012. *ProQuest*, proxygwa.wrlc.org/login?url=https://search-proquest-com.proxygwa.wrlc.org/docview/1022981275?accountid=33473.

367 "PEABODY ANNOUNCES DOCUMENTARY, EDUCATION WINNERS."*US Fed News Service, Including US State News*, Apr 27, 2016. *ProQuest*, proxygwa.wrlc.org/login?url=https://search-proquest-com.proxygwa.wrlc.org/docview/1784422565?accountid=33473.

368 Staff, Billboard. "Who Are All the Girls in Maroon 5's 'Girls Like You' Video?" *Billboard*, 31 May 2018, www.billboard.com/photos/8458698/maroon-5-girls-like-you-video-every-woman.

369 Defillo Ana. "Beyond Borders." *Teen Vogue*, vol. 16, no. 4, 05, 2016, pp. 94-n/a. *ProQuest*, proxygwa.wrlc.org/login?url=https://search-proquest-com.proxygwa.wrlc.org/docview/1786260821?accountid=33473.

370 *Common Cause v. Biden*, 909 F. Supp. 2d 9 (2012).

371 Valdes, Marcela. "STAYING POWER: IS IT POSSIBLE TO RESIST DEPORTATIONS IN THE AGE OF TRUMP?"*New York Times Magazine*, May 28, 2017, pp. 50–56,6. *ProQuest*, proxygwa.wrlc.org/login?url=https://search-proquest-com.proxygwa.wrlc.org/docview/1903442397?accountid=33473.

372 Bowen, Robert. "ICE Releases Dream Activist's Mother and Brother; Why The Arrest to Begin With?" *The Examiner*, 11 Jan 2013, www.examiner.com/article/ice-releases-dream-activist-s-mother-and-brother-why-the-arrest-to-begin-with.

373 Santos, Fernanda. "After Immigration Arrests, Online Outcry, and Release." *New York Times (1923-Current file)*, Jan 12, 2013, pp. 1. *ProQuest*, proxygwa.wrlc.org/login?url=https://search-proquest-com.proxygwa.wrlc.org/docview/1814933225?accountid=33473.

374 AP, Immigration activist joins US Rep. Sinema's staff, Jan. 17, 2013.

375   Foley, Elise. "Erika Andiola: Stop Deportations First, Then Fight For Legislation." *HuffPost*, 5 Dec. 2013, www.huffpost.com/entry/erika-andiola-deportations_n_4386412.

376   Terris, Ben. *Staffer Leaves Hill to Stop Mom's Deportation.* Atlantic Media, Inc, Washington, 2013. *ProQuest*, proxygwa.wrlc.org/login?url=https://search-proquest-com.proxygwa.wrlc.org/docview/1465060493?accountid=33473.

377   Carrasquillo, Adrian. "Prominent DREAMer Erika Andiola Arrested While Supporting Hunger Strikers In Arizona." *BuzzFeed News*, 26 Feb. 2014, www.buzzfeednews.com/article/adriancarrasquillo/prominent-dreamer-erika-andiola-arrested-while-supporting-hu.

378   "14 Things the President Could Do to Improve Immigration Policy That Don't Require a Change to Any Laws." *#Not1More Deportation*, www.notonemoredeportation.com/2014/04/10/not1morebrc/.

379   Linan, Ali. "UPDATE: 15 DACA Recipients, Protesters Detained After Pro-Immigrant Rights Sit-in Outside Texas Capitol." *TCA Regional News*, Jul 26, 2017. *ProQuest*, proxygwa.wrlc.org/login?url=https://

search-proquest-com.proxygwa.wrlc.org/
docview/1923451308?accountid=33473.

380 Sands, Geneva. "This Year Saw the Most People in
Immigration Detention since 2001." *CNN*, Cable News
Network, 13 Nov. 2018, www.cnn.com/2018/11/12/
politics/ice-detention/index.html.

381 8 U.S.C 1182(a)(9).

382 Jackson, Reagan. "Maru Mora-Villalpando in Her
Own Words." *The Seattle Globalist*, 5 Nov. 2018,
www.seattleglobalist.com/2018/10/22/maru-mora-
villalpando-in-her-words/77959.

383 Now!, Democracy. " 'ICE Is Sending Us a Message':
Activist Maru Mora Villalpando on Being Targeted for
Deportation." *YouTube*, 17 Jan. 2018, www.youtube.com/
watch?v=uQiIV6xjQ2g.

384 "Maru Mora Villalpando: Support the Immigrant Hunger
Strikers! Stop the Deportations!" *Revolution Interview
Maru Mora Villalpando: Support the Immigrant Hunger
Strikers! Stop the Deportations!*, revcom.us/a/334/
maru-mora-villalpando-support-the-immigrant-hunger-
strikers-stop-the-deportations-en.html.

385 Villalpando, Maru Mora. "ICE Came After Me, and
I Fought Back." *Law at the Margins*, 25 July 2018,

lawatthemargins.com/ice-came-after-me-and-i-fought-back/.

386 Ibid.

387 "700 Immigrants on Hunger Strike at For-Profit Prison to Protest Conditions & $1/Day Wages." *Democracy Now!,* www.democracynow.org/2017/4/14/700_immigrants_on_hunger_strike_at.

388 Jones, Liz. "She Says Her Activism Put Her on ICE's Radar." *KUOW*, 25 Oct. 2018, kuow.org/stories/she-says-her-activism-put-her-ice-s-radar/.

389 Villalpando, Maru Mora. "ICE Came After Me, and I Fought Back." *Law at the Margins*, 25 July 2018, lawatthemargins.com/ice-came-after-me-and-i-fought-back/.

390 James, Will. "Northwest Activist, Facing Deportation, Heads To Trump's State Of The Union." *KNKX*, www.knkx.org/post/northwest-activist-facing-deportation-heads-trumps-state-union.

391 Tichenor, Daniel. "The Historical Presidency: Lyndon Johnson's Ambivalent Reform: The Immigration and Nationality Act of 1965."*Presidential Studies Quarterly*, vol. 46, no. 3, 2016, pp. 691–705. *ProQuest*, proxygwa.wrlc.org/login?url=https://

search-proquest-com.proxygwa.wrlc.org/
docview/1819108266?accountid=33473, doi:dx.doi.
org/10.1111/psq.12300.

392 Raff, Jeremy. "The 'Double Punishment' for Black
Undocumented Immigrants." *The Atlantic*, Atlantic
Media Company, 3 Jan. 2018, www.theatlantic.com/
politics/archive/2017/12/the-double-punishment-for-
black-immigrants/549425/.

393 Rivas, Jorge. "This man is leading the fight to blackify the
undocumented immigrant rights movement." *Splinter
News*, 7 Jul. 2016, splinternews.com/this-man-is-leading-
the-fight-to-blackify-the-undocumen-1793860574

394 Ibid.

395 *Van Hollen, Cardin, Feinstein, Kaine Introduce
Legislation to Protect TPS Recipients*. Federal
Information & News Dispatch, Inc, Washington, 2019.
ProQuest, proxygwa.wrlc.org/login?url=https://
search-proquest-com.proxygwa.wrlc.org/
docview/2197622252?accountid=33473.

396 DeChalus, Camila. "Ph.D. Student Faces Deportation
to Liberia, Where She has Never Lived." *Roll
Call*, Mar 18, 2019. *ProQuest*, proxygwa.wrlc.org/
login?url=https://search-proquest-com.proxygwa.wrlc.
org/docview/2193401298?accountid=33473.

397   Flynn, Meagan. "Federal Judge, Citing Trump Racial
       Bias, Says Administration Can't Strip Legal Status
       from 300,000 Haitians, Salvadorans and Others—for
       Now." *The Washington Post*, WP Company, 4 Oct.
       2018, www.washingtonpost.com/news/morning-mix/
       wp/2018/10/03/federal-judge-citing-trump-animus-
       against-nonwhites-blocks-removal-of-haitians-
       salvadorans-and-others/?utm_term=.59e3e95b7ecc.

398   Hoo, Stephanie. "Those Who Suffer most." *The
       Progressive*, vol. 82, no. 6, Dec, 2019, pp. 23.
       ProQuest, proxygwa.wrlc.org/login?url=https://
       search-proquest-com.proxygwa.wrlc.org/
       docview/2161261392?accountid=33473.

399   Frej, Willa. "Woman Who Scaled Statue of Liberty
       was Protesting Trump's Immigration Policies:
       Therese Patricia Okoumou was Apprehended After
       She Climbed Up the Statue and Stayed on it for a
       while." *ProQuest*, Jul 05, 2018, proxygwa.wrlc.org/
       login?url=https://search-proquest-com.proxygwa.wrlc.
       org/docview/2081808529?accountid=33473.

400   Walters, Joanna. "'Are They Going to Shoot Me?': Statue
       of Liberty Climber on Her Anti-Trump Protest." *The
       Guardian*, Guardian News and Media, 7 July 2018, www.
       theguardian.com/us-news/2018/jul/07/statue-of-liberty-
       protester-patricia-okoumou-interview.

401   Walters, Joanna. "'I Must Continue': Statue of Liberty
      Climber Still Protesting despite Facing Prison." *The
      Guardian*, Guardian News and Media, 13 Dec. 2018,
      www.theguardian.com/us-news/2018/dec/13/patricia-
      okoumou-statue-of-liberty-protester-trial-new-york-
      federal-prison.

402   Lind, Dara. "The Trump Administration Just Admitted
      It Doesn't Know How Many Kids Are Still Separated
      from Their Parents." *Vox*, 5 July 2018, www.vox.
      com/2018/7/5/17536984/children-separated-parents-
      border-how-many.

403   Brown, Stephen Rex, et al. "Statue of Liberty Protester
      Patricia Okoumou Sentenced to 5 Years' Probation."
      Nydailynews.com, New York Daily News, 19 Mar.
      2019, www.nydailynews.com/new-york/manhattan/
      ny-metro-liberty-protester-probation-20190319-
      trkfkcyysfajbdd3nt6lofrbya-story.html.

404   Elfrink, Tim, and Fred Barbash. "'These Children Are
      Barefoot. In Diapers. Choking on Tear Gas.'." *The
      Washington Post,* WP Company, 26 Nov. 2018, www.
      washingtonpost.com/nation/2018/11/26/these-children-
      are-barefoot-diapers-choking-tear-gas/.

ABOUT THE AUTHOR

● ● ● ● ● ● ● ● ● ● ●

A leading scholar and expert on immigration law and policy, Prerna Lal was born in the Fiji Islands, came to the United States with their parents when Lal was fourteen, and grew up in the San Francisco Bay Area, California.

Formerly an undocumented immigrant, Lal was integral in the establishment of advocacy networks led by undocumented youth, and mobilized thousands of undocumented immigrants into pushing for the federal DREAM Act in 2010, ending the deportations of undocumented youth, and winning the now popular Deferred Action for Childhood Arrivals (DACA) program from the Obama Administration. Lal also helped with the creation of many local immigrant youth groups—providing direct support, mentorship, and advocacy to individuals caught up in the immigration dragnet.

As an undocumented law school graduate, Lal was among the first in the country to obtain a license to practice law. Their high-spirited activism also made them a target of the US government who sought to deport Lal (2010–2014), but Lal won lawful permanent residency after a long court battle. In April 2018, Lal became a United States citizen.

As a non-profit policy attorney in Washington DC, Attorney Lal worked at Asian Americans Advancing Justice—AAJC to craft federal policies such as extended DACA, DAPA, Temporary Protected Status (TPS) for Nepal and parole-in-place for the family members of Filipino war veterans (all of which are now under attack by the Trump Administration). Most recently, Attorney Lal served as the sole immigration counsel for over five hundred students and their family members at the University of California, Berkeley, single-handedly creating and sustaining the first school-based legal services program in the United States. At the East Bay Community Law Center and UC Berkeley School of Law, Lal taught at the immigration law clinic and mentored a new generation of public-interest law students.

Lal has previously contributed to books such as *Undocumented and Unafraid: Tam Tran, Cinthya Felix, and the Immigrant Youth* and *The Country I Call Home*. Lal has also penned articles for *The New York Times*, *HuffPost*, *TruthOut*, *New America Media*, *In These Times*, and has been quoted in hundreds of news outlets in the United States and abroad.

Prerna Lal now owns and manages their own law firm, Lal Legal, where they continue to serve immigrants and shape immigration advocacy. They live in Berkeley, California.

ABOUT MANGO

• • • • • • • • • •

Mango Publishing, established in 2014, publishes an eclectic list of books by diverse authors—both new and established voices—on topics ranging from business, personal growth, women's empowerment, LGBTQ studies, health, and spirituality to history, popular culture, time management, decluttering, lifestyle, mental wellness, aging, and sustainable living. We were recently named 2019's #1 fastest growing independent publisher by *Publishers Weekly*. Our success is driven by our main goal, which is to publish high quality books that will entertain readers as well as make a positive difference in their lives.

Our readers are our most important resource; we value your input, suggestions, and ideas. We'd love to hear from you—after all, we are publishing books for you!

Please stay in touch with us and follow us at:

Facebook: Mango Publishing

Twitter: @MangoPublishing

Instagram: @MangoPublishing

LinkedIn: Mango Publishing

Pinterest: Mango Publishing

Sign up for our newsletter at www.mango.bz and receive a free book!

Join us on Mango's journey to reinvent publishing, one book at a time.